Accomplices of Silence

The Modern Japanese Novel

MASAO MIYOSHI

Accomplices of Silence

The Modern Japanese Novel

UNIVERSITY OF CALIFORNIA PRESS
BERKELEY · LOS ANGELES · LONDON

University of California Press
Berkeley and Los Angeles, California

University of California Press, Ltd.
London, England

Copyright © 1974 by
The Regents of the University of California

ISBN: 0-520-02540-7
Library of Congress Catalog Card Number: 73-83062
Printed in the United States of America

To Kathy, Owen, Melina,

Their Sister-in-Law C.-C.

And the Mother of Them All

Contents

Preface

The modern Japanese novel or *shōsetsu* is now nearly one hundred years old. From the very start, it was predominantly Western in impulse as writers turned away from the traditional tales and romances and actively sought new narrative forms to fit the new Age of the West. A literary program gradually took shape: the new fiction would attempt to deal with the ordinary experience of ordinary people and would be written in a colloquial language from the average person's moral perspective. An impossible program, as we will see, and yet by now, after almost a century, there is a distinct sense shared by many Japanese writers that the novel, once an imported art, has been successfully naturalized. What is more, Japanese novelists tend now to talk quite comfortably about their work in the context of the great nineteenth- and twentieth-century Western novels, *Crime and Punishment* and *The Trial*, *Ulysses* and *Remembrance of Things Past*. We can say then that there exists a tradition of the Japanese novel which is formally as well as thematically recognizably "universal," at least in intent.

While it is true that Japanese writers would not have conceived the *shōsetsu* without having fairly close acquaintance with Western literature, this is not to say that in developing the *shōsetsu* they totally abandoned their own tradition, with its distinct logic-style and sensibility built right into the images and vocabulary, the setting and the argument. The ancient goals and values of the people could not be reconstructed overnight, nor, obviously, could the long strands of personal and tribal memory woven into the very sound and syntax and semantics of their language be identified, excised, and replaced in the span of a generation or two. In short, somewhere in the substance of each modern piece of Japanese literature lies an element native to the core and as such utterly intransigent and unreconstructible.

Clearly, such cultural and artistic grafting processes involved in generating a new literature give rise to wide discrepancies between program and execution, theory and the pulse of experience, and they must be understood if we are to get hold of some of the difficulties as well as the achievements of the modern Japanese novel.

I would like at this point to summarize the argument of the book since the plan for the following chapters—each devoted to a particular author and his works—does not allow for coherent discussion of such material. There will be a focus on four basic aspects of the art of fiction—the narrative situation, character, plot, and language—but radiating out from these points are a range of other problems which will be explained and elaborated more fully in the book itself.

I see it as impossible to discuss the narrative situation without treating the notion of character. The story must be told by someone, and the author must choose a voice for his storyteller. In so doing, he inevitably conceives of his narrator as a character, too, thus involving his whole understanding of human personality. And yet, in almost every novel—*The Drifting Clouds, Through the Dark Night,* or *No Longer Human*—we notice something decidedly loose, or overcasual, in the narrative plan. Often, the narrator telling the story is the author's undisguised personal pre-literary self. Or, we may find him choosing to speak through a surrogate character whose mask is nonetheless transparently thin. Often, too, the grammatic person shifts around very freely from first to third, and from one first-person speaker to another first-person speaker. More importantly, we see everywhere—even in Sōseki—a free shift in the point of view, and even in the narrative mode, from the third-person novel to the first-person diary, confession, or letter. It used to be easy to regard the unstable point of view as a sign of a naïve or clumsy art, as Percy Lubbock did in his blanket judgment on all pre-Jamesian novelists. But this won't help us much now when the Jamesian "point of view"— premised on the alienation of the individual, the unbridgeable gulf separating each one of us from the other—is recognized as itself an assumption.

Like the author, the Japanese critic, too, usually pays little heed to the narrative situation. With the exception of Nakamura Mitsuo writing on Shiga Naoya or Etō Jun treating Sōseki, the critics ignore the possibility of voice problems, and concentrate instead on the so-called philosophy of the master novelists. This general indifference to the tale-teller's identity points to the still present belief in a communal storytelling persona that can slip into any story and take on the voice of an undifferentiated narrative self. *Who* tells the story doesn't seem to matter much; it's the action that counts.

Any discussion of the narrative situation thus quickly turns into the question of character in the novel. But before I go on to discuss "character," let me emphasize the importance to this study of those extraliterary essays on the Japanese personality by people like Nakane Chie, Ruth Benedict, Edward Norbeck, Inatomi Eijirō, and Herman Kahn, who have stressed, as I do, that the Japanese attitude toward personality (not any particular trait, but "personality" itself) is basically profoundly negative. The self, that cornerstone of European humanism, is of course academically understood, but is nowhere felt as an everyday experience. The Japanese *Bildungsroman* is not so much about the self's discovery of the self as the self's discipline of itself into a production model hierarchically classified and blueprinted in detail by society at large. And this is so whether we are speaking of Ōgai's *Youth*, Sōseki's *Sanshirō*, or Tōson's *Spring*.

Concomitant to this notion of the self as a production unit is the fact that the characters in the Japanese novel are almost always types, and not living individuals. Thus, one may easily recall situations, scenes, or relationships of characters (say, Kan'ichi and Omiya in *The Golden Demon*, or Shinji and Hatsue in *The Sound of Waves*), but seldom oneself experience intimacy with a character, as one does with Emma or Heathcliff or Isabel Archer. However interesting and absorbing Futabatei's Bunzō, Sōseki's *sensei*,

Kawabata's Shimamura, Dazai's Naoji, or Mishima's Mizoguchi, still they are abstracts finally, markers of the plot-logic, and not portraits of real people. As such they are almost literally bound into the context of their books and simply can't be seen clearly in relief apart from the narrative. We are always aware of the author's fascination with them, but almost never get to grapple with them as real people with their own existence.

This quality of character seems to spring from the same source as the narrative problem: the obscure outlining of the self in the Japanese novel. Although the writer is often preoccupied with questions about "the I and the Other" (with a capital O), this is not the same as "the I and many diverse others." That is, the culture's control of individual awareness reinforces belief in a collective, metaphysical entity, The Other. The traditional novel, woven as it is from the relationships of several individuals, does not thrive in such an absolutist milieu, and so the I-novel (*shishōsetsu*) comes to dominate, replacing the pluralist "real world" with a private universe. The "I-novel" is thus not just one genre among many, but the essential pattern of Japanese prose fiction toward which even the most panoramic social novel gravitates. It is somewhat ironic, surely, that the "*I*-novel," the autobiographic retelling of the author's very personal life, should grow out of a myth of the collectivized self, and not of one celebrating individual personality.

The more we look at it, plot, too, begins to relate to character and narrator traits. We might talk first about serializing, the mode of publication which came to prevail in Japanese fiction. Take Futabatei, who published *The Drifting Clouds* at random intervals over a long period, or Kawabata, whose *Snow Country* and *The Sound of the Mountain* came out unpredictably over several years in different journals, as well as many of today's writers who serialize in various journals. With these writers, as with the Victorian novelists—most conspicuously, Dickens—serialization is both cause and effect of their imaginative makeup: their creativity actively seeks out serialization as a preferred mode every bit as much as the mode then determines the curve of the plot. Either way, novelistic coherence is not the writer's main purpose. Flaubert and James, George Eliot and Joyce, each in his own

way carves out a verbal sculpture which goes far toward convert-
ing the novel's temporal art into a visual, spatial structure. The
Japanese writer, on the other hand, stops and starts the narrative
flow, and uses tension between passages and their crucial placement to propel his story, which will often leap from one episode
to another (see, for instance, Kawabata's later works, particularly
those in which the spirit of *renga* is so powerful).

In the traditional Western novel the plot coheres by virtue of
the carefully laid network of causal relationships. We can see an
egalitarian aspect to this causality, since the expected patterns of
action, made reasonably explicit in the fictional context, apply
to everyone universally, regardless of circumstance. And it has a
bourgeois aspect, given that prose fiction, being middle class in
origin, rejects the heroic whereas clearly the romance and the epic
do not. And finally it is commonsensical, redolent of everyday life.
With such features of the novel in mind, we see that the Japanese
novel contrasts rather sharply with its Western counterpart, primarily because it tends to distrust this egalitarian impulse and
disdain a commonsense explanatory system. Thus for every *Light
and Darkness,* there are hundreds of *The Setting Sun*s, which belong more naturally with the romance, the lyric, the confession,
and such. *The Setting Sun,* like other typical Japanese novels, has
very little plot: events occur, but with no explicit moral or causal
interpretations to account for them. And the Japanese novel still
celebrates the hero's victory or glorifies the anti-hero's defeat, as
in so many novels by Mishima Yukio, a writer who in his own
person was a consciously created hero (or anti-hero) in a heroless
age.

Now to language, which is probably the most significant element in any discussion of Japanese fiction. First, there is the
noticeably large divergence between the spoken and the written
language. Of course, this is not uniquely a feature of the Japanese
language; even in American literature, it was only with Mark
Twain that the gap between speech and "book talk" began to
narrow. In Japanese, however, this gap was immense in the early
Meiji years, almost to the extent of there being two distinct stages
of linguistic development—as that, say, between Middle English
and modern English. *Bungo* (the written style) was refined but

remote; *kōgo* (the spoken style) was familiar but vulgar and certainly no proper medium for art. Gradually a compromise—a sort of dignified colloquialism—was worked out. But even at that, the characters in these "compromised" works did not talk like real people, and the narrative passages came out stiff and quaint. Perhaps the problem is bigger than just that of colloquialism, or "how to write as you speak": it may have something to do with the visual nature of Chinese ideograms as a writing system, or with the stylized speech patterns of ordinary life. Whatever the main reason for it, the remoteness of the *shōsetsu* language seems to place prose fiction at a distance from real life even now.

The next feature of the novelistic language, the system of honorifics (*keigo*), is more important than is usually recognized. In actual conversation *keigo* operates so as to establish immediately the relative social standings of speaker, listener, and referent. This carries an advantage for the novel, providing as it does a calculus of social class that even Jane Austen might have envied for its precision and freedom from ambiguity. And yet there are difficulties. For instance, the narrator must choose a level for himself in relation to the reader. In the early Meiji years, when the social role of the writer was still unfixed, the choice of the *-desu* suffix system over the *-da*, or vice versa, presented him with an agonizing problem in composition. Here too a compromise was negotiated; in this case a neutral level, neither deferential nor condescending, was invented which solved some problems but of course introduced others. For the "neutral" level has no real counterpart in conversational usage; it is strictly an artificial language, for use in fiction alone and thus ultimately itself a fiction also.

There are also both advantages and disadvantages in the floating tense, loose syntactic form, and the like. The vague tense system, for instance, allows for subtlety and ambiguity: in Sōseki's *Pillow of Grass*, the intricate shifting between present tense and past creates an impressive play of its own. However, when the narrative requires expository clarity, it resorts to the stiff "translation style" invented for handling the Western literatures. This style sounds artificial, and it is, imposing a distance between fiction's world and the actual world. Mishima's works, for instance, often have to suffer from this appearance of affectation only because the author is trying to establish a plain discursive narration and there seems no other way to get it than "translation style."

Perhaps more important than any other factor in this whole problem of language and style is the typical Japanese dislike of the verbal. It might be said that the culture is primarily visual, not verbal, in orientation, and social decorum provides that reticence, not eloquence, is rewarded. Similarly, in art it is not articulation but the subtle art of silence that is valued. *Haiku* is the most perfect embodiment of this spirit but it is visible elsewhere as well. Thus the novel, that loquacious art, needs some trimming to fit the Japanese verbal dimensions. By and large, the Japanese novel is very short and only rarely approaches the average Victorian three-decker. In fact, the term *shōsetsu* is applied to both the full-length "novel" and the short story as though no difference existed. But aside from length, this passion for silence is in evidence in the narrator's attitude toward the story. Often, the scene of the Japanese novel is set by suggestion and evocation rather than description. At its best—as in Kawabata's *The Sound of the Mountain*—this silence fairly resonates with meaning. At its worst (Mushakōji Saneatsu's proverbs and platitudes or Dazai's baby-talk), the writer is clearly embarrassed by his articulation. On the other hand, when the writer who is well aware of this power of silence still defies it outright, as does Haniya Yutaka in much of his work, the result is often a torrent of intellectualisms without reference to experience, and thus a nearly unreadable work.

I do not believe it an overstatement to say that writing in Japanese is always something of an act of defiance. Silence not only invites and seduces all would-be speakers and writers, but is in fact a powerful compulsion throughout the whole society. To bring forth a written work to break this silence is thus often tantamount to the writer's sacrifice of himself, via defeat and exhaustion. If A. Alvarez is right in seeing an essential relationship between modern literature and suicide, the modern Japanese novel and its authors are surely the most representative case: all three writers discussed in Part Two took their own lives. In the course of the book, I will consider some of the probable causes of this situation, which seem to me inherent in the whole Japanese attitude toward both art and language, and as such, they are closely related to, if not wholly identifiable with, Alvarez's explanations. The discussion of the formal features of art and language will lead out intrinsically to such "life" problems.

The Japanese novel, then, does not conform to the specifications of the Western novel on which it is modeled. But that in itself should not bother us. We are aware that during this century of *shōsetsu* development, lots of things have been happening to the Western novel, too. Robbe-Grillet, Nabokov, and Norman Mailer belong to a different tradition from that of George Eliot. And indeed, the demise of the novel of Fielding and Tolstoy, James and Hawthorne, that has been whispered for some decades is now past history. The new antinovels are distinguished by plotlessness, the disintegration of character, and a deliberate dislocation in the narrative situation. Thus, if the Japanese novel finds no place near the traditional Western novel, one can comfortably think of *Pillow of Grass* or Kawabata's more "Japanese" works in the company of these new Western antinovels. Natsume Sōseki sensed this quite early, in 1905, when he called his *Pillow of Grass* a plotless and eventless *"haiku shōsetsu"* and pointed out how entirely new the work was in the context of the Western novel. Looked at this way, the novel, an imported art to begin with, has at last naturalized itself to Japanese.

Of the six writers discussed in the book, three are old masters of the Meiji and early Taishō era (around the turn of the century), which saw the first flowering of modern Japan. The other three all belong to the reign of Hirohito (from 1926), who presided over the rise and catastrophic fall of his Empire and is now witnessing the rise of an economic empire not inappropriately referred to in some quarters as "Japan, Inc." The six are at the forefront of those who have charted the course of Japanese prose fiction: Futabatei wrote what is considered the first modern Japanese novel, whereas Mishima marks a very special climax in recent literature. Certainly there are others: Izumi Kyōka, Shimazaki Tōson, Shiga Naoya, Nagai Kafū, Tanizaki Junichirō, Yokomitsu Riichi, Abe Kōbō, and Ōe Kenzaburo. And yet these six in many ways better represent the landmark achievements as well as the difficulties and failures of Japanese fiction.

For each of the six there is an intensive discussion of one or two works, all available in English. As for the choice of these novels, I have no rationale other than my prejudice, with the qualification that this is always endorsed by the existence of a good-to-excellent English translation. Apparently, at least in these instances, my preferences and the translators' seem to coincide.

The book is meant principally for the general reader of novels. Twenty years ago it most probably would not have been thought of: with the exception of Arthur Waley's classic translation of *The Tale of Genji* and occasional translations of *haiku* and *noh* plays, on the encouragement of Yeats or Pound, Japanese literature was almost totally unknown outside Japan. Since then, however, a number of Japanologists—Howard Hibbett, Donald Keene, Edwin McClellan, Earl Miner, Ivan Morris, Edward Seidensticker, and several others—have made the Japanese novel so accessible to the English-speaking reader that knowledge of at least a few Japanese works can now be expected from just about everyone who likes to read and think about modern literature. Although I assume no knowledge of the language in the reader and have made my references in English wherever possible, there are, to be sure, an increasing number of students of Japanese who no doubt prefer to check certain details for themselves against original versions of the novels and the native scholarship. For such scholar-students I have devised and placed at the back of the book a second set of notes referring to bibliographical matters, secondary materials, or the details of Japanese words and phrases requiring *Nippon-go no chishiki*. Apart from these notes, the only section of the book that might conceivably task the English-only reader is the first half of the first chapter where I discuss the problems the prose fiction writers faced in dealing with the Japanese language a century or so ago.

I am grateful for the fellowship I received from the John Simon Guggenheim Memorial Foundation and for the Humanities Research Professorship from the University of California, grants which enabled me to complete this manuscript in a relatively short time. My thanks are also due to Mark Schorer and Nathan Glazer for nudging me forth from my habitat of Victorian literature.

Many friends and colleagues have read the manuscript at various stages, giving me innumerable helpful comments, and I am especially in debt to John Anson, Earl Miner, Carolyn Porter, Edward Seidensticker, Wayne Shumaker, and Henry Nash Smith.

It must have started a long time ago, well before I began seriously to read Japanese literature myself, that I began to encounter American readers of Kawabata and Mishima, Tanizaki and Sōseki who seemed to know exactly what they wanted to read and who read it astonishingly well. I was continually struck by their ways of looking at this "exotic" literature, but I was also necessarily reminded of the translators who had made the novels accessible to such readers over the last few decades. Without the work of this skilled and dedicated cadre offering a glimpse of a "world elsewhere," these readers would never have emerged, and there would scarcely exist any reason for this book. Knowing how difficult it is for foreigners to learn the language, I am indeed indebted to their splendid work.

Berkeley   MASAO MIYOSHI

Acknowledgments

Thanks are due the following for their permission to use passages from the works indicated:

Poems by Wallace Stevens, edited by Samuel French Morse. Copyright © 1959 by Wallace Stevens. Reprinted by permission of Alfred A. Knopf, Inc.

Kawabata Yasunari's *The Sound of the Mountain,* translated by Edward G. Seidensticker. Copyright © 1970 by Alfred A. Knopf, Inc. Reprinted by permission of Alfred A. Knopf, Inc.

Arthur Waley's *The No Plays of Japan.* Copyright © 1957 by George Allen & Unwin Ltd. Reprinted by permission of George Allen & Unwin Ltd.

Harold G. Henderson's *An Introduction to Haiku.* Copyright © 1958 by Harold G. Henderson. Reprinted by permission of Doubleday & Company, Inc.

Sylvia Plath's *Ariel.* Copyright © 1965 by Ted Hughes. Reprinted by permission of Harper & Row and Olwyn Hughes.

The Penguin Book of Japanese Verse, edited and translated by Geoffrey Bownas and Anthony Thwaite. Copyright © 1964 by Geoffrey Bownas and Anthony Thwaite. Reprinted by permission of Penguin Books Ltd.

Note on Japanese Names

Japanese names throughout the book (except my own) are written in Japanese order—surname first—the style Japanologists have adopted in their studies in English. In Kawabata Yasunari, for example, Kawabata is his family name, and Yasunari his given (or "first") name. Even when the writer adopts a sobriquet (such as Futabatei Shimei), this order is followed. To complicate things, however, writers are known in Japan sometimes by their surname and sometimes by their "given" name. Natsume Sōseki (Natsume Kinnosuke) and Mori Ōgai (Mori Rintarō), for instance, are usually known as Sōseki and Ōgai, not as Natsume and Mori, whereas more recent writers like Dazai Osamu (Tsushima Shūji) and Mishima Yukio (Hiraoka Kimitake or Kōi) are known as Dazai and Mishima. It seems that as a writer comes to be accepted into the "great tradition" (usually a while after his death), he comes to be known more by his given name than his surname. This book follows the current usage in this regard.

Part One

So still:
    into rocks it pierces—
        the locust shrill.
          —BASHŌ

Only shape thou thy silence to my wit.
        —Twelfth Night

To the music of the reaper's flute
No song is sung
But the sighing of wind in the fields.
        —SEAMI, *Atsumori*

        Denn das Schöne ist nichts
als des Schrecklichen Anfang, den wir noch grade ertragen,
und wir bewundern es so, weil es gelassen verschmäht,
uns zu zerstören. Ein jeder Engel ist schrecklich.
        —RILKE, *Die Erste Elegie, Duino 1912*

Has the Garden of Silence been already lost? Then
    birds must arm themselves.
        —HARAGUCHI TŌZŌ, *Etudes I*

I

THE NEW LANGUAGE

THE GEMBUN'ITCHI MOVEMENT
—*Ban Japanese, and speak English.*

In Tokyo in 1886, several writers decided to circulate their manuscripts among themselves in order to exchange ideas and develop some sense of audience. Their "journal" was a very modest venture; it was not even printed at first but copied in a very neat hand. Calling themselves the Friends of the Ink-Pot (*Ken'yūsha*), most were not more than twenty years old, their birth just about coinciding with the accession of the Emperor Meiji, who was then engaged in his vast program of restructuring the nation. The journal, humorously called the *Rubbish Library* (*Garakuta Bunko*), has a historical significance far greater than most publications of its kind.[1] As with other movement papers (for example, the *Germ* of the Pre-Raphaelites around 1850), its artistic execution fell somewhat short of its intention. The work published in the *Rubbish Library* did not elevate Japanese fiction to a very serious level, nor did it do much to purify the language. Despite this, it claims our attention.

One of the key members of the club was a precocious seventeen-year-old, Yamada Bimyō, whose literary program, published in the third issue of the *Rubbish Library*, condemns the whole development of the Meiji novel, scoffing at its practitioners as mere popular entertainers. In another (unpublished) essay he even

attacks Edo (or, interchangeably, Tokugawa) masters like Kyokutei Bakin, Ryūtei Tanehiko, Tamenaga Shunsui, and Juppensha Ikku, contrasting the low and vulgar state of the Japanese
novel with the situation in Western countries where the form is
taken seriously by writers as well as by the vast novel audience.
His examples of Western "novelists" do indeed constitute a mixed
bag: Voltaire, Rousseau, Spenser, Shakespeare, Milton, and Cer-
vantes. Had he named instead the late-Victorian popular writers,
his argument would of course not have held. At any rate, he did
set up a program for himself that called for no less than the "improvement of literature," and, in fact, of the language itself. If
the manifesto sounds to us today somewhat sophomoric, Bimyō's
diagnosis of the novels of the time was nonetheless cogent. Those
of the earlier Meiji years—from 1870 on—were basically no more
than rehashings of the Edo conventions. And although the younger
writers were beginning, along with Bimyō, to bring in some new
thematic elements via adaptations of Jules Verne or Disraeli, they
also definitely felt the need for a language that could express the
new ideas and new life style they were seeking.

In the Preface to his novel *A Note on the Organ* (*Fūkin Shirabe
no Hitofushi*), which was serialized in a feminist magazine in
1887, Bimyō is quite specific in his analysis:

> Ever since someone argued that the correspondence be-
> tween spoken and written languages was a good proof of
> civilization, people have begun to worry about the style of
> our language. But we still have a great enemy in habit and
> inertia. Any new and unfamiliar style provokes people
> preoccupied only with the surface of things and invites
> their negative comments like "vulgar" and "inelegant."
> In the face of these charges, no one dares to try the col-
> loquial style exclusively. Especially as regards the novel
> of manners, the dialogue is barely "vernacular" enough,
> and yet the narrative portions retain the "elegant style"
> characterized by the *-nari*, *-keri*, and *-beshi* suffixes. This
> inconsistency between dialogue and narrative within the
> same novel is really unsightly. We must remove it no mat-
> ter how difficult the task may be. Some people seem to be

giving up the idea of matching spoken and written styles as hopeless in present-day Japan. But they are too impatient. Of course, the elegant style may have something that colloquialism does not; but in the hands of a skilled writer, colloquialism can offer an indescribable gracefulness with a discipline all its own, which is in no sense inferior to the elegant written style. It is from this perspective that this novel was written: in short, in the style, somewhat modified, of the love stories as recited by the *yose* storyteller Enchō.[2]

What Bimyō is talking about is generally known by the term *gembun'itchi* (the correspondence between spoken and written languages), which he coined around that time with other writers including Mozume Takami, a professor of literature at the University of Tokyo. In fact, Bimyō was only one of a growing number of writers at the time who expressed great concern over the state of the Japanese language. Not only critics and novelists, but editorial writers and even the government demanded some method whereby legal documents and commercial and personal correspondence could be brought linguistically closer to the vernacular. The barrage of earnest responses included one advocating adoption of the Roman alphabet, and another urging total abolition of Japanese and substitution of English.* It is no accident, therefore, that a month before *A Note on the Organ* began to appear, one of Bimyō's childhood friends, Hasegawa Tatsunosuke, was writing the first part of his novel, *The Drifting Clouds (Ukigumo)*, one of the central concerns of which was the discovery of a new language for the novel.

Before introducing Futabatei Shimei (as Hasegawa was to call himself), we must examine the formidable *gembun'itchi* program, since it is fundamental to our understanding of the new novel of the time and, in some important respects, to our understanding of the modern Japanese novel right up to the present.

---

* This innovative proposal was made in 1872 not by a lunatic but by Mori Yūrei, who later became minister of education for the central government. Yamamoto Masahide, *Kindai Buntai Hassei no Shiteki Kenkyu* (Tokyo: Iwanami Shoten, 1965), p. 117.

Readers who do not understand Japanese may point out here that the adoption of colloquialisms into the novel is a relatively recent event even in English, not to mention other Western languages. Certainly it is true that in the great majority of nineteenth-century novels the characters still do not speak like "real people." Take Thackeray or Meredith, Hawthorne or Melville, George Eliot or even Henry James: their characters, however "vivid," observe a certain decorum in their speech as well as in their behavior, as stipulated by the conventions of the novel. With Twain's *Huckleberry Finn,* and, in a more general sense, with Gertrude Stein and Hemingway, the dialogue and even the narrative voice for the first time attempt to reproduce authentic speech.[3] But the experience of the Japanese novel is entirely different in this matter, not at all comparable to the too formal syntax of a Jane Austen, the overly abstract exposition of a George Eliot, or the too "poetic" stylization of a Dickens. The discrepancy at that time between spoken Japanese and the language of the novel resembled the difference between two historical stages of a given language, say, Old or Middle English and modern English.

This of course raises the question as to how far back one should go in tracing this divergence between spoken and written speech. The usual explanation starts with the contrast between the Edo and the Meiji novel, but this seems to me to suggest more questions than it answers.[4] It makes more sense to go back all the way to the time around the fourth century when Chinese ideograms were first being introduced as a medium of writing into the largely unlettered Japanese language.[5] The Japanese manner of importing the written characters was ingenious. Once having appropriated the ideograms of a language linguistically totally unrelated to their own, the Japanese gave them native pronunciations. An ideogram expressing *mountain,* for instance, was pronounced "yama," the Japanese sound signifying *mountain.** Yet while this "naturalization" of ideograms was being carried out rapidly and on a very large scale, the Japanese was also borrowing directly from the

* The nearest analogy to this method of borrowing is the use of Arabic numerals by various languages. The figure "1," for instance, is pronounced as "one," "Ein," "un," "ichi," and so on, although the sign itself does not change.

Chinese sounds. Thus, an ideogram ordinarily had—and still has
—at least two different pronunciations, Japanese and Chinese,
with little difference in the meaning, although the borrowed Chinese
sound itself was of course naturalized by adjusting its phonetic
components.* For example, the ideograms expressing *Japan*
were—and still are—pronounced as "Nippon" and "Nihon" (Chinese)
and "Hinomoto" (Japanese); even the name of the novelist
Kawabata Yasunari is very often pronounced "Kawabata Kōzei"
(or "Kōsei"), despite his preference for "Yasunari." Some confusion
was inevitable, and is still in evidence in the process by which
the Japanese child learns the language, not to mention the adult
foreigner.

But the matter is still more complicated. Since Chinese and
Japanese are not linguistically related, the Chinese written medium
could not fully meet the needs of the Japanese language.
Hence, the Japanese of those early centuries soon began to use
ideograms as phonetic symbols. Because Chinese ideograms number
in the tens of thousands, sound notation by such means was
extremely cumbersome. By the eighth century the Japanese were
somehow managing to write out traditional lore and poetry by this
method in the *Kojiki* and *Nippon Shoki* chronicles and in the great
Man'yōshū anthology of poems. To ease the matter somewhat, a
more rational phonetic use of ideograms was also invented by
this time: instead of applying more than one ideogram for each
sound, only one was chosen to represent any one sound, and the
writing of that ideogram itself was simplified by reducing the
number of strokes. Thus came into being the *kana* system of
syllabic writing with 47 characters for the principal 47 syllables
of the language.†

---

* Actually, the situation is more complex. The Chinese sound for a given ideogram
did not remain constant throughout history. At different stages, different
sounds (for the same ideogram) were imported, being each time adjusted to the
Japanese phonetic properties. To make the situation worse, dialectal variants were
also transmitted. Thus, many "Chinese" sounds can exist for one ideogram.

† Actually, two systems of *kana* were developed, *katakana* and *hiragana*. The
distinction between the two is not easy to put, but the former is used more limitedly
in the *kambun* notation—or, more recently, for the expression of Western words
—while the latter is for more general use. This statement requires one more qualification:
the sound structure of ancient Japanese was far more complex (as has been

The literature of the Heian period (794–1185) was written either in Chinese ideograms alone or in *kana* interspersed with ideograms. The ideographic text, called *kambun* (strictly, "writing of Han"), looks like Chinese but is not pronounced like it. A *kambun* text, as read by a Japanese, sounds Japanese and is Japanese, although it could also be read by a Chinese and pronounced in Chinese.* Compared with *kana,* the *kambun* style was felt to be more learned and dignified, and, reflecting the Japanese aspiration for Chinese culture, the male courtiers and scholars appropriated it for government documents and for, by and large, a banal poetry highly imitative of the Chinese sources. The *kana* style, considered less learned, was delegated for the use of the sex of weaker mind. Interestingly, quite apart from any feminist persuasion I might have in this matter, it is the *kana* writings of this time, represented by Lady Murasaki and Sei Shōnagon, that make it one of the greatest periods in the history of Japanese literature. The *kambun* style, written exclusively in ideograms, has survived in the way a dead language survives, to torment high school students who must pass the *kambun* requirement in their curriculum.

The *kana* style thus overcame the *kambun,* at least where literary expression was concerned. Yet the mixture of *kana* and ideograms does not necessarily guarantee a more Japanese style than the use of ideograms alone. And this peculiarity of Japanese typically using a compound writing system—foreign ideograms and native syllabary—is important to the understanding of *gembun'-*

---

shown by Hashimoto Shinkichi) than that of modern Japanese, and had many more *kana* letters expressing these now extinct vowels and consonants.

* To give an illustration, suppose that English now, instead of Chinese centuries ago, were introduced to an unlettered Japan. (Keep in mind that English and Chinese have a roughly similar word-order.) It would operate like this: The native sentence, *Konya wa umi ga shizuka desu,* would be written down as "[The] sea is calm tonight," but would be pronounced in Japanese as "Tonight sea calm is," by transposing the written characters. To ease the reader's adjustment, a system of notations must be devised, looking somewhat like this: Sea[2] is[4] calm[3] tonight.[1] With Chinese ideograms being largely non-phonetic, the job was slightly easier than this example might suggest. (I am not quite sure that I have made the matter clearer by this example, but hopefully something of the complicated process is conveyed.) Incidentally, for centuries Japanese learned to read Chinese literature itself by this method of Japanizing via notation, and the same method was used by the earlier teachers of English.

itchi. For one thing, until very recent times, the *kambun* style has always formed the core of academic and bureaucratic orthodoxy. This does not mean that government documents, for instance, were always written exclusively in ideograms; they usually employed both ideograms and *kana*. And yet, the tone, diction, and even syntax of *kambun* were so dominant that they constituted an identifiable literary style, *kambun-tai* (or *-chō*), even where the text was written out in the *kana*-ideogram mixture. So stereotyped was this style that for centuries it effectively worked against any significant integration of the changing patterns of speech with the writing. Second, this process has meant the absorption into Japanese of a very large portion of the classic Chinese vocabulary. It is practically impossible to write Japanese without using Chinese "loan" words in quantity—no more possible indeed than to write today's English exclusively in old Saxon. The borrowed words are clearly much more deeply entrenched in the written vocabulary than in the spoken, and the less familiar (and less "naturalized") ones are those found mostly in the written vocabulary.* Thus, the more lofty and elegant the writing (the more "Chinese"), the more alien it is to everyday Japanese. Third, there is the problem of intelligibility. Japanese is phonetically very limited, and there are innumerable homophones indistinguishable one from another unless identified by appropriate ideograms. The sound "shi," for example, can mean "teacher," "samurai," "city," "history," "Mister," "capital," "four," "stop," "death," "poetry," and many other things. Use of only the *kana* for this sound, without the help of an ideogram, creates a hopeless

---

* It is quite possible for the speaker of Japanese to recognize the rough meaning of a given ideogram without knowing for certain how to pronounce it, which is another way of saying how visual the Japanese language is, compared with, say, Germanic or Romance languages. In this connection, it may be of some interest to observe that the Japanese writer is very conscious about the appearance of the printed page. Japanese are almost always trained in the art of calligraphy, and what an ideogram looks like as a design, or how the mixture of *kana* and ideograms on a page strikes the eye, is in fact a serious matter. There is hardly any counterpart to this in the West—except perhaps in Mallarmé, certain seventeenth-century writers of shaped poetry, and, lately, Robert Creely (who is heavily influenced by Japanese poetry). Mishima Yukio, among others, talks about this phenomenon in his *Manual of Style (Bunshō Tokuhon)* (Tokyo: Chūōkōronsha, 1970), pp. 23–26. See my discussion of Sōseki's *Pillow of Grass* below.

confusion in communication, even where the context might provide some direction. The fact of phonetic poverty has thus further
deepened the gulf between spoken and written language. Written
documents, meant primarily to be read silently, not read aloud,
or heard, carry a reduced risk of ambiguity. But a speech or other
text intended to be read aloud requires a vocabulary and style
quite different, since immediate intelligibility is of the essence.
Last, all these factors together have contributed toward the establishment of a powerful expectation that stylization (decorum, convention, stereotype) will be observed in written documents of all
kinds from personal letters to fiction to government publications
—even today in the last third of the twentieth century.*

By the time the young Meiji writers began searching for an
appropriate style, Japanese literature had fifteen hundreds years'
experience of using ideograms and *kana* together. Thus the question was not how best to blend the two, but how to forge a new
writing style out of the various styles already in use, each associated with a different proportion of ideograms and *kana:*
kambun-tai, which depends heavily on ideograms; *gabun-tai*
(elegant style), which also uses them heavily, although its syntax
is looser and its vocabulary more native; *zokubun-tai* (vernacular
style), which, in its attempt to capture true speech patterns, relies
very much on *kana;* and *gazoku-setchū-tai* (elegant-vernacular
mixed style), which tries to combine the last two.

Historically, such a variety of styles indicates the fascinating
sociology of the language. Traditionally, the *kambun-tai* and
gabun-tai both have belonged to the aristocracy and have reflected
the learned and graceful culture of the few who cling to the
ancient manners on which their social distinction so largely de-

---

* This may be one of the reasons skills in public speaking are so underdeveloped
in Japan. Most speeches on ceremonial or public occasions, for example, are no
more than readings of prepared texts (written often in a quaint style) with little
consideration for the audience. (Emperor Hirohito's broadcast announcement of
the surrender in 1945, for instance, was practically unintelligible to most listeners.
They were not certain until they read the text later whether the Emperor ordered a
cease-fire or an out-and-out battle to the end.) Similarly, deficiencies in elocution
are often a serious problem for all who speak in public, even actors. One tentative
solution is the increased stylization of speech, which Westerners may recognize in
Japanese films and in *kabuki* plays.

pends. But during the three-centuries-long Tokugawa period (1603–1867), when Japan was virtually sealed off from the rest of the world and was under the control of the Shogunate, the merchant class was steadily accumulating wealth and political power. And with the gradual rise of this new "middle" (that is, non-samurai) class,* came its own cultural expression. The *kabuki* play, the *haiku* verse form, the *jōruri* recitations, and the novel were the arts of this new class, just as the *noh* play, the *waka* verse form, and *kambun* typified the samurai class. Given the fact that the Japanese language is highly diversified as to class dialects (even now any Japanese can tell one's class background with dead accuracy just from certain vocabulary and suffix-style habits), the literature, too, of the middle classes began to reflect their speech habits with increasing confidence. Especially in the novel, a form which thrives in a democratic milieu, they very boldly recorded the accents and manners of their own speech.[6] Ihara Saikaku (1641–1693) and then Juppensha Ikku (1765–1831), Shikitei Samba (1776–1822), and Tamenaga Shunsui (1789–1843), instead of merely copying the elegant language of the imperial courtiers and samurais, made full use of the more casual, informal speech of the Edo and Osaka burghers, which soon developed into the so-called vernacular style.[7]

Even so, these early novelists were not entirely free of the stereotyped learned language. At its core, the Edo novel, like any other novel tradition, shows time after time the characteristic middle-class hankering after the grace and charm of the aristocracy. Thus did Kyokutei Bakin (1767–1848), for example, use *kambun-tai* almost exclusively to write about those fantastic super-heroes of his whose appeal was not primarily to the samurai class but to the growing number of tradespeople and their families. And other writers, too, chose for the most part to reconcile their impulse toward accurate representation of what they know with the dictates of decorum by writing elegant-formal narrative parts

---

* This is a most inexact term. The increase in capital during the Tokugawa period accelerated steadily, and some merchants in Osaka, Kyoto, and Edo were as wealthy as many of the great lords (*daimyō*). Thus, I am referring here simply to the consciousness of social caste that remained very much intact despite the redistribution of wealth.

interspersed with vernacular-mimetic dialogue. In short, the narrator in these novels assumes an elegant voice for himself, while
providing his characters with the everyday speech of the ordinary
people the writer himself has no doubt come from.[8] The compromise worked to a degree because the typical reader, accustomed to
plays and *yose*-stories (quasi-epic *kōdan* and comic *rakugo* recitations, for example), condescendingly responded to the dialogue
as if watching a vulgar performance, while trusting the narrator
to describe and interpret it from the loftier moral and artistic position presumably shared by his audience.

The early Meiji writers, Futabatei, Tsubouchi Shōyō, and the
Friends of the Ink-Pot, such as Bimyō and Ozaki Kōyō, learned
the technique of vernacular dialogue from reading Samba, Shunsui, and other Edo writers, but they could no longer accept the
stylized narrative alongside it, as the quotation from Bimyō
shows. Verisimilitude was important in narrative too and they
were determined to find a style that would suit the whole novel,
not just the dialogue.

Another important problem for the *gembun'itchi* movement was
the use of the "honorific" (*keigo*), which is basic to any consideration of the narrator's language. For the foreigner, the honorific
system, with its "levels of reverence," is probably the most baf-
fling grammatic feature of Japanese. Actually, *keigo* has little or
nothing to do with politeness in the Western sense. Sometimes also
called "status expression" (*taigū hyōgen*),[9] it can be defined as
the expression of degrees of reverence, or irreverence, depending
on the relative positions of speaker, listener, and referent. A
speaker adopts a reverential level if his listener (or his referent)
is superior to him in class, employment, age, and so forth; an
irreverent level, if inferior; or any of a number of levels in between, according to the class relationships. Of course, there is
something similar to this even in English ("Get the hell out!" as
against "Would you mind leaving, sir?" for instance), but nothing
in the Western languages comes near the prominence and perva-
siveness of the honorific system operating in Japanese. The suffix
(and sometimes prefix) of almost every verb and the prefixes of
most nouns must be adjusted to signify the relative positions of

the three poles involved in speech utterance, and the vocabulary requires sensitive selection, particularly among the personal pronouns. The scrupulous but automatic choice of level operates continuously in speech—even, it should be noted, where the statement concerns neither speaker nor listener (such as "Socrates is mortal" or "It's a holiday today"). The native speaker of Japanese almost reflexively sizes up any new acquaintance within seconds of their first social interaction. Of course, even in a society so steeped in the arts of defining relative "altitude," an occasional pair of near-equals will appear, their honorific level being largely determined by their common social role. By and large, between young male equals, each speaks as though the listener were his inferior (less polite); between female equals, each speaks as though the listener were her superior (more polite); between male and female equals, she speaks with reverence, he without it, as can be expected of a society confirmed in its centuries-old male chauvinism.

In the traditional *kambun-tai* and *gabun-tai* writing styles the honorific system has been somewhat neutralized over its long history (perhaps as a result of high stylization), whereas in the spoken style, reflecting the rigid social stratification established during the Tokugawa period, it is still extremely elaborate. If a novel is to be in the vernacular, therefore, it not only must reproduce the honorific system in the relationship of characters, but also must choose a proper level between narrator and reader. Here, however, there is no tradition, no history, no ready convention to guide the choice. Should the narrator speak respectfully to the reader, as if the reader were patronizing the *yose* hall? Or should he adopt the tone of a lofty teacher to his lowly pupil? Or should he after all assume a more democratic level? Obviously, the precise ground of the narrator-reader relationship can be determined only if the novelist, his art, and his readers are all defined in social and cultural terms. If the writer would be an intellectual, a modern bard and prophet presenting a more or less comprehensive picture of reality, he will take a lofty tone, and he may be revered as a master. If on the other hand he is a mere entertainer trifling in inanities, he had better speak humbly. But whether prophet or entertainer, the question is, who is his audience? * During the early years of the novel, writers were very hesitant about their social-linguistic position vis-à-vis their readers, and there was a great deal of experimentation. For instance, Bimyō and Futabatei tried the reverential -*desu*, -*dearimasu* suffix system as well as the more casual -*da*, -*dearu*. But most writers around this time, whenever they felt strain, tended to retreat into the formalized territory of the archaic *kambun-tai* and *gabun-tai*.

The characters' speeches presented a further problem to the *gembun'itchi* program. Here, I must discuss things more generally to include the thematic aspect of the Edo novel. Very much like eighteenth-century European fiction, the novel of the Edo period falls into categories: picaresque (Asa Ryōi, *Ukiyo Monogatari,* 1650s; Ihara Saikaku, *Kōshoku Ichidai Otoko,* 1682); gothic (Ueda Akinari, *Ugetsu Monogatari,* 1776); semi-pornographic, describing the pleasure quarters ("Yellow Books" by Santō Kyōden and others; Shunsui, *Shunshoku Umegoyomi,* 1832; Saikaku's works); the epic romance (Bakin, *Nansō Satomi Hakkenden,* 1814–41); and humor (Shikitei Samba, *Ukiyo Buro,* 1809–12; Juppensha Ikku, *Tōkaido Hizakurige,* 1802–9).[10] They gloried in the exploits of quasi-mythical figures, or chuckled patronizingly at goings-on in the world of geishas and prostitutes and their clients. They were in turn didactic, sentimental, or farcical, but they seldom explored behind the external behavior of men and women. Above all, none were noticeably concerned with the ordinary moral and psychological processes of ordinary men and women that are always the main territory of the novel.

Indeed it would have been noticeable to have been concerned at all. The Edo period is psychologically almost medieval. Japanese society had been so tightly bound all those centuries by a hierarchic structure in which feudal and religious values domi-

---

* A somewhat similar uncertainty is discernible among English writers of the nineteenth century. See, especially, Wordsworth's Preface to the *Lyrical Ballads.* In the novel, though, one can easily think of various relationships between writers and their reading public (which was becoming identifiable and "respectable" in England for the first time in the last half of the nineteenth century) in the period between, say, Austen through Dickens to Henry James.

nated that an unquestioned code of behavior—chivalry (*bushidō*)
for samurai, face and obligation (*memboku* and *giri*) for the tradesmen, and decorum for all—was the only guide for conduct. Life's
ongoing activities were undisturbed by any rapid infusion of new
cultural values, and such an infusion, as in the Meiji period, with
its resulting moral and psychological dislocations, was still un-
dreamt of. On the rare occasion when some strange shock of self-
recognition brought a darker view of life, a writer could still be
consoled by other attitudes such as *wabi, sabi,* and *iki*—the kind
of aesthetic nirvana afforded by Buddhism and the development
of exquisite taste in the theater and other arts.[11] It was not until
the Meiji Restoration—no radical revolution certainly, and yet an
undoubted transformation of samurai and merchant classes alike
into the efficient managerial bureaucracy which is the basis for
today's Japan, Inc.—that the sine qua non of the novel, the looser
society that individualizes and introverts man, began to take form
in Japan. Modern bourgeois life, for all its ills, at least allows man
to look at himself for a time while he interacts with others outside
his immediate family and community. Modern man drifts along
his own path in a cool and expanding universe, but such sparse
worlds alone seem to generate the novel. Take Sōseki's *Light and
Darkness (Meian)*—it would have been as unthinkable in pre-
Meiji Japan as a *Vanity Fair* by a twelfth-century Englishman.

Thematic changes might ordinarily be thought to have little to
do with aspects of language and style. At this stage of the Japanese novel, however, there were several reasons why the two must
be looked at together. For one thing, the Meiji period had come
up with many new ways of mixing people traditionally separated
by geography and social position. (As was noted earlier, the Japanese language is highly diversified vertically as well as geographi-
cally.) The Edo novelists, involved in their samurai exploits or
with their geishas in the pleasure quarters, saw only part of the
problem, as in Juppensha Ikku's comic travelogue where two dudes
travel down the Tōkaidō highway and run into some bumpkins.
The Meiji novelists faced a new kind of relationship with the
multiplicity of social subgroups, the students, the housemaids, the
civil servants, the "downtown" merchants, the day laborers, all of
whom had their own more or less distinct speech patterns. Could

they include all this diversity in their writing, thereby breaking the decorum expected of their "elevated" art? Or would they instead idealize the distinct speech styles in various ways, thereby muting the radical differences?

Even more important was the new outlook on life and society that came with the introduction of Western culture. It is hard to keep in mind that a mere hundred years ago so many words crucial to the conduct of life in present-day Japan were simply not in coin: almost all political terms, Western philosophical concepts, names of Western imported objects; all the Japanese equivalents for, say, democracy, train, equality, idealism, and trousers. The words had to be coined as the concepts or objects were introduced. And the neologisms had to be negotiated into literature with all the uncertainties of intelligibility, connotation, and propriety that this implied. Especially when English and other European words were directly incorporated, the uncertainties were bound to increase, causing writers to worry a great deal about accuracy in the process of Japanizing the sound and sense—as once, centuries before, they must have worried when borrowing massively from Chinese. Insofar as a novelist was concerned with depicting contemporary scenes, he could not evade the job of somehow, either by approximation or new coinage, finding words for Western ideas and things. Even now the difficulty is very acute, neology being one of several serious problems for the Japanese novelist; at the beginning of the novel tradition it must have been immense.

The discovery of the Western novel was both the cause and the effect of the powerful impulse toward verisimilitude in the language of Japanese fiction. Since most modern Japanese writers could read some English, and occasionally French, German, and Russian, the translation of European novels began to flourish with a vigor unknown anywhere outside Japan. Futabatei and Mori Ōgai were both translators, and Natsume Sōseki was a professor of English. Clearly the consideration of which style to use for the translation of a Bulwer novel or a Shakespeare play was bound to yield new stylistic suggestions for the direction of the Japanese novel itself, leading directly to the challenge proposed in the name of *gembun'itchi*.

The issues involved in the *gembun'itchi* program faced every writer during those early years of the novel, whether he articulated a position on them or not, and are far from settled even for writers of the present day. Futabatei, the first modern Japanese novelist, took the first important steps toward confronting them.

"DROP DEAD": THE WRITER'S IMPERATIVE FUTABATEI SHIMEI: *THE DRIFTING CLOUDS*
—*Futabatte shimei.*

There are two facts about Futabatei Shimei (1864–1909) that are important in connection with *The Drifting Clouds* (*Ukigumo*), certain circumstances of his education, and his friendship with Tsubouchi Shōyō.[12] Futabatei was born in Tokyo, still called Edo, in 1864, four years before the Meiji Restoration of the emperor's rule. His father was a low-ranking samurai, a fact that would be insignificant except that his status was both low enough to allow absorption of much of the old burgher culture and high enough to ensure his son's enrollment in a traditional samurai school. Futabatei grew to love *kiyomoto, shinnai, tokiwazu,* and *jōruri*—various types of recitation accompanied by the guitar-like *samisen*. These musical narratives—which are, incidentally, extremely difficult to read, not to say listen to—were vital transmitters of Edo culture, and Futabatei learned from them all the pathos and irony of the Edo people while familiarizing himself with a language very similar to that of the older novels. In the schools he first attended in the home town of his clan, the curriculum was largely Chinese classics (in *kambun*), and he was steeped in the Confucianism that for centuries had been the basis of samurai education. But the clan's official school, like many others at the time, also offered French and English instruction, and Futabatei learned enough French to understand what it means to know a foreign language, while tasting for the first time literary tidbits from the exotic West. By the age of seven, Futabatei had some real experience of a different culture.

His Western studies were accelerated in 1881 when he entered the Tokyo Foreign Language School, an extraordinary institution in its time and even by today's standards. In the Russian Department where he was enrolled, the entire curriculum from physics and chemistry to literature was conducted in the language to be learned, many courses being taught by Russian émigrés who knew very little Japanese. The writers Futabatei read while still a schoolboy made up an impressive list, including Pushkin, Lermontov, Turgenev, Gogol, Goncharov, Tolstoi, and Dostoevsky. It was a far cry indeed from the teaching of languages in present-day Japan, where students learn how to translate a foreign language into Japanese, but seldom the reverse, and almost never how to speak it—which is exactly the old *kambun* method of Japanizing a foreign language.

Futabatei kept up a lifelong relationship with Russian literature. First, his translations from Turgenev, Gogol, Goncharov, and others, published from 1888 on, are far more accurate and sensitive than any other translations of those days when Shakespeare's plays and *Tales from Shakespeare* were virtually interchangeable.[13] His renderings reproduce the original sentence unit, carefully preserving the verbal texture, rhythm, and tone together with the accurate meaning of each word.[14] The style he adopts, furthermore, is remarkably colloquial. "The Tryst" (*Aibiki*) from Turgenev's *A Sportsman's Sketches,* which he published in July–August 1888, between the second and the third installments of *The Drifting Clouds,* is simple in syntax, fresh and graceful in expression, and largely native in vocabulary. Above all, the narrator's tone is surprisingly neutral despite its *-da, -dearu* suffix system, which in the hands of a lesser craftsman would have fallen crude and coarse on Meiji ears. In his translation of a Gorky story, on the other hand, the rough speech of a laborer is matched in Tokyo workers' vernacular. Futabatei learned from his Russian translations whatever can be learned from the style of a modern European text: consistency in the narrative tone, a brief and clear syntactic structure, the craft of *le mot juste,* the true rendition of actual speech. The application of such techniques to his own writing is clearly in evidence in the later parts of *The Drifting Clouds*.

Second, Futabatei wrote many essays throughout his career on various literary subjects—the art of fiction, style, *gembun'itchi*, translation, and Russian literature. Most are newspaper or magazine pieces, quite brief (only a few pages), and often conversational, and none amount to a developed treatment of any single subject. But scattered among these are his astute observations and impressions concerning literary practice, and especially his preoccupations with *le mot juste,* which he learned from Turgenev's well-chiseled art. As for his broad and deep knowledge of the Russian novelists, it was far ahead of anyone else's in those days. In "The Standards of My Translation" (*Yo ga Honyaku no Suijun,* 1906), he confides that all the praise or blame he received for his translations was pointless and irrelevant, and that all along his critical struggle was largely with himself.

Finally, Futabatei's knowledge of Russian literature opened new thematic horizons. In "A Chat on Russian Literature" (*Roshia Bungaku Dan*), for instance, he discusses the lineage of the Oblomov character in Russian novels. He sees the man who would stay in bed all day to avoid an uncomfortable draft in terms of the conflict between the old Russia and the new Western European culture which fragmented and polarized the values and identity of the intellectual. Although Futabatei does not refer in this essay to the analogy between nineteenth-century Russia and Meiji Japan, it is clear to anyone who has read *The Drifting Clouds* what he had in mind in the essay.

Futabatei met Tsubouchi Shōyō (1859–1935) in January 1886, a few days after he withdrew from the Foreign Language School. Shōyō, only five years older than Futabatei, was already a rising figure in the literary world. Fresh out of the prestigious University of Tokyo, he had already published translations of Scott's *The Bride of Lammermoor* and *The Lady of the Lake,* Shakespeare's *Julius Caesar,* Bulwer's *Rienzi,* and had written *The Essence of the Novel (Shōsetsu Shinzui)* and several works of fiction, of which *The Temper of Today's Students (Tōsei Shosei Katagi)* was the most important. Although Futabatei's respect for Shōyō was deserved, their relationship, which lasted until Futabatei's death in 1909, was not one of a teacher-pupil sort. On the subject which brought the two together, fiction and the language of fiction, it was always the younger and lesser known of the two who had the wider knowledge and clearer grasp of the problem. In fact, scholars are unanimous in regarding Shōyō's later turn from creative work to teaching and translation as being largely the consequence of his friendship with Futabatei which made him realize the limitations of his own talent.

The Temper of Today's Students (1885–86) was a new novel in its own way. Presenting the student scene of the early Meiji years, it documents some interesting aspects of middle-class student life: money worries, experience in the red-light district, and slang largely made up of English, German, and French words (as it still is today). But aside from the novelty of the setting, the work is as vapid as most of its contemporaries. The plot follows a series of impossible machinations that would shame even a Bulwer: Shōyō claimed it was modeled on Thomas Hughes's *Tom Brown at Oxford* and Thackeray's *Pendennis,* but it does not merit even those rather modest comparisons. The work is actually a rehash of the Edo pleasure-quarter novels, substituting students for tradesmen. Its language is even more disappointing: the intrusive and extravagant narrator depends heavily on stereotypical epithets, puns, and formulas that by this time had become purely extrinsic ornaments, and in moments of excitement falls into a 5–7 meter (roughly comparable to Dickens' blank verse). Perhaps its main contribution to the novel was the prestige that Shōyō, a respectable university man, lent the craft of novel writing, at that time still considered a rather low and vulgar occupation.

The Essence of the Novel (1885–86) is quite another matter. Here Shōyō is determined to formulate a systematic overview of the art of fiction. Since no native criticism of any significance was available to him to organize his ideas,[15] he had to borrow from English and American journals (the *Nineteenth Century* and *Forum,* for instance), the *Encyclopaedia Britannica,* several textbooks of rhetoric, and lectures by visiting professors such as Ernest Fenollosa.[16] "The Novel as Art," "The History of the

Novel," "The Subjects of the Novel," "The Kinds of the Novel," "The Benefits of the Novel"—such are the headings of the first half of the 200-page volume. The main thesis in this section is the independence of the novel from overly didactic concerns. Verisimilitude, not *kanzen chōaku* (reward virtue, punish vice), is its primary function, according to Shōyō. In the course of his discussion, he blames Bakin and all the Edo novelists and praises Richardson, Fielding, Scott, Bulwer, Thackeray, and George Eliot, about whom, however, he has very little to say in support of his praise. And despite his anti-didactic position, Shōyō quietly reintroduces the notion of morality by pointing out that the effect of reading a novel is elevating by definition. Unfortunately, he does not argue this rather intriguing point thoroughly enough.

The second half of the treatise is devoted to discussions of style, plot, and character in the novel, the historical novel, and other such specific subjects. The chapter on style is fairly significant. Here Shōyō talks about the elegant style (*gabun-tai*), the vernacular style (*zokubun-tai*), and the elegant-vernacular mixed style (*gazoku-setchū-tai*), saying very much the same things as Bimyō was to say soon afterward except that he is more tentative in his recommendation of colloquialism. The elegant style is too effeminate and remote to be the language of the novel; the vernacular style, on the other hand, too local and familiar. His choice falls on a compromise, the mixed style, at least for the present. What is most interesting is his expression here of an urgent hope for the emergence of "some talented man who could find a way of removing all these shortcomings of colloquialism." [17] Little did he know—this Shōyō, already one of the brightest men of his time and soon to become the greatest Japanese translator of Shakespeare—that the talent he called for in this book already existed in his new friend Futabatei Shimei. This circumstance, together with the fact of his own disappointing performance in *The Temper of Today's Students* (which he apparently believed exemplified his ideas of the novel), suggests a great deal about the still inchoate condition of the novel, as well as Shōyō's limitations as a theorist of literature.*

* Despite its vagueness, however, Shōyō's essay is impressive enough for its time: after all, even in England the general discussion of the novel was just about to

Futabatei gave Shōyō a draft of *The Drifting Clouds* in the latter part of 1886 and asked him for suggestions on improving it. The master liked it pretty much as it was, but at the same time —as he later came to regret—advised the young writer to elevate the tone by increasing the Chinese vocabulary in certain passages.[18] Futabatei apparently accepted this wrong-headed advice and made repeated revisions of the work. Shōyō then handled the arrangements for publication even to the extent of lending his name as co-author.

It is at this point that the young author's pen name, "Futabatei Shimei," was adopted. A name such as this—a slightly modified form of "futabatte shimei," the equivalent of "drop dead," *—was fairly unusual at a time when most writers, following the custom of the old Chinese and Japanese men of letters, chose elegant names like "Shōyō" (Wanderer), "Kōyō" (Red Maple Leaf), and "Bimyō" (Beauty and Mystery). Futabatei later confided in his friend that the name was his father's reaction to his decision to make a career of writing. Elsewhere he recorded his shame at having leaned on his teacher's name to get his work published, a self-hatred also expressed very exactly in the pen name.[19] Clearly, the name tells something about this brilliant young man, who was always honest and ironic about himself, to the point of serious self-doubt. It also suggests, in a broader context, the alienation expressed by other writers who felt themselves cut off from the mainstream of the society by contemptuous or embarrassed family members or friends.

The Drifting Clouds, Part One, was published in June 1887; Part Two, completed some time toward the end of the year, was published in February 1888; Part Three, the last, was serialized in July and August 1889 in a biweekly magazine. The exact date of the completion of the last part is not clear, but it was probably

---

begin around this time with James, Robert Louis Stevenson, Walter Besant, and others. And with the exception of George Henry Lewes, there is no one earlier who set forth a coherent treatment of the novel

* I mean the *sound* of the name, the ideograms chosen to fit the sound being elegant and self-ironic: the ideograms for "Futabatei" mean "cottages of two leaves" (the first two leaves of a seedling) and those for "Shimei," "four perplexities" (*mei* means "to be lost," "to go astray"). Marleigh Ryan's inaccurate translation of the name as "go to hell" denies its significance.

around July 1889 (after the beginning of the serialization). As was the case with many Victorian novels, serialization was not then unusual in Japan, nor is it now. It should be stressed, though, that the degree of reader accommodation is often minimal in this sporadic kind of serialization, quite unlike that in a Dickens serialization. Also it should be kept in mind that Futabatei's novel was written and published over a fairly long period of time with the consequence of considerable change in its verbal features.

The title, *Ukigumo,* is evidently intended to suggest the hero's uncertain position relative to both his love and his position in society. Besides "drifting," *uki* can be read as either "sad" or "gay," depending on which ideogram is used. When spoken, *uki* at once sets off the paradox inherent in the pun. Also, *ukiyo* (floating world) is a key term in Edo literature, and the most representative arts of the period are called *ukiyo-e* (pictures of the floating world, chiefly woodcut prints), and *ukiyo-zōshi* (stories of the floating world, or the novel).[20] Futabatei's choice of this title, then, at once signifies the tradition he has inherited, while also pointing to the essential ambivalence of sadness and gaiety, tragedy and comedy (or the *carpe diem* of Edo decadence and Buddhist resignation) quite evident in the work itself.

The novel is brief (less than 150 pages in the standard text), which is often the case in Japanese fiction, and the plot, unlike that of Shōyō's novel, is extremely simple. The young man in the story, Bunzō, is laid off from his government job. His aunt Omasa, in whose house he lives, is annoyed and begins to show her contempt for him. Bunzō is in love with his cousin Osei, but the beautiful girl's reaction to this news is rather indefinite. Bunzō has a worldly and aggressive colleague, Noboru, who presents a threat to his marital prospects. What fills the story is the day-to-day family conversations, Bunzō's unending self-analysis, and a few episodes such as Bunzō's efforts to find another job, and Noboru's visit, in the company of Omasa and Osei, to a chrysanthemum show. The chronology of the narrated events is also very short: less than two weeks (October 28 to November 8) in the first sixteen chapters and a few subsequent weeks in the remaining three.

A simple story with a very brief chronology can indicate either trivialization—which is not the case here—or the internalizing of events. And for the author to have worked hard at it for nearly three years suggests the possibility at least of his continual assessment and reassessment of his material. The work is thus doubly psychological in the sense that, while exploring the inner experience of the main characters, it also reveals the author's fluctuating feelings about this experience. And the temporal structure of the novel, reflecting this psychological complexity, is far from simple.

The story opens with a conversation between two men just after one of them has been given notice of dismissal. As yet unnamed, they are singled out from the rush-hour crowd of office workers and government bureaucrats hurrying home. The next two chapters flash back to fill in the background of the man who was fired: his now deceased father, formerly a samurai, his impoverished and helpless mother, his energetic aunt, his beautiful cousin with whom he is in love, and so on. After that, the narrative progression more or less straightforwardly covers the rest of the short duration. Yet a clear outline of the passing time is not what the reader perceives. For one thing, the "events" of the novel are to such a degree internal that, despite numerous temporal references, it is impossible to mark the calendar. Then, too, the portrayal of the vacillating and pusillanimous young introspective is necessarily a little tedious. One reflection leads to another, still to another, then turns back to the original point, such circularity defeating the projection of any clear sense of passing time and in any case retarding the novel's tempo by lengthening the felt time. There is also the matter of grammatical tense. Japanese has no clearly established tense, and forms for past and present are often interchanged without creating any confusion for the reader. *The Drifting Clouds* is for the most part written in such a past-present mixture, and this, though it might on occasion intensify reader involvement in the manner of the "historical present," usually tends to obscure the linear time development. (The author himself is apparently halfhearted in tracing the passage of time, since the very first sentence contains an error: "at 3 p.m., the twenty-eighth of October, leaving only two days to the end of the month." And there are other discrepancies: in chapter 9, for example, "fifth day [since October 28]," ought to read "seventh day."

As for the repetitiousness, it, too, is deliberate. Take the four successive descriptions of Osei in the first four chapters. The first time the reader hears about her, in chapter 1, she is merely referred to as "your sweetheart" by Noboru. In the same chapter, the housemaid reports to Bunzō how Osei looked earlier that day when she went out with her mother. The description is largely of her clothes and not of her total appearance and expression. In the second chapter, the reader is given a brief account of her schooling and Bunzō's growing love for her, but no direct portrayal. In the next chapter, the reader comes a little closer; she is now reported as Bunzō sees her—as it happens, under the moonlight. A full daylight account of her appearance must await chapter 4, where the narrator attempts to provide a more objective view, though in no less admiring terms. The effect of this is twofold. First, the process by which the reader is introduced to Osei parallels the way one often comes to know another person in real life. Second, the narrative sequence at the same time disrupts the chronology of the events. Chapters 1 and 4 belong to the same day, while chapters 2 and 3 deal with the past. All of this means, simply, that our progress in coming to know Osei does not accord with ordinary temporality, and thus our grasp of the plot is somewhat obscured.

Such temporal obfuscation, however, is not necessarily a disadvantage: in this novel, especially, whose chief movement is "drifting," the absence of a clear linear progression is almost a formal requirement. Even the author's abandonment of definite time references in the last three chapters helps create a sense of temporal dislocation which is the expected consequence of drifting.

This discussion of the novel's narrative sequence leads naturally, I believe, to the question of the language in which the narrative is set forth. The most important feature is the archaism that dominates a fair proportion of this "new" novel. Here is a passage from chapter 2 as Marleigh Ryan* translates it:

> Bunzō was so happy he could have danced for joy. He had been terribly overworked by his aunt since coming to her house and had, in addition, very much disliked his role

* Unless otherwise indicated, the quoted passages are from the translation in Marleigh Grayer Ryan, *Japan's First Modern Novel: "Ukigumo" of Futabatei Shimei* (New York and London: Columbia University Press, 1967).

as a dependent nephew. Now that he was back in school, he was able to devote his full time and energy to his studies without any distractions.

But even at school he was continually reminded of his poverty and loneliness. He had no one to spoil and pamper him as the other boys had, no one to give him an allowance. He channeled all his youthful energies into his studies. He was inspired by an overwhelming desire to bring joy to his destitute mother and to repay his great debt to his uncle by being successful at school. And he was. He took either first or second place—but never lower —in every examination. He was the pride of his teachers. His rich and lazy fellow students were very jealous of him. (Pp. 206-7)

A perfectly ordinary style, as any translation probably ought to be, but the original is hardly so plain and clean. In fact, the whole of these two paragraphs is originally only one sentence which runs—at the risk of incoherence—like this:

Till yesterday, in the misery of being but a hanger-on at [his] uncle's home, being slave-driven and anxious, even frightened, to please; today, no longer ordered around by anyone, now able to devote his entire time and energy to study, well, wasn't [he] pleased, so pleased, that [he] jumped up and down in pleasure; but a student though [he] is now, it too being also a life of troubles; of course unlike the spoilt rich sons, having no fancy treats like help from parents, [he] cannot waste even a penny, but then doesn't want to; only being determined that [he] must relieve his helpless, lonely mother, must pay back his uncle for the debt; [his] study—undertaken in struggle and hard work with no wasted time—advancing remarkably; always being ranked the best, not even the second, at every examination; teachers being impressed [by him] as an extraordinary student.*

It may be remarked here that since systematic punctuation in

---

* My rendering is from the Iwanami Shoten edition of the *Complete Works,* I, 11-12 (see note 19).

Japanese was, in a sense, a new concept developed only a short while earlier, and Futabatei may not yet have learned its full use or significance, it may be a mistake to take his commas and periods too seriously. At the same time Futabatei did learn the concept of syntax from his foreign-language study, as his sentence-by-sentence translation of "The Tryst" will bear out. Besides, archaism can be an advantage. The loose sentence, which he inherited from the *yose* storytellers and the Edo *gabun-tai* writers, while clearly unsuited to precise statements requiring definite syntactic relationship of subject and predicate, is remarkably effective here where the hero cogitates seemingly endlessly and without explicit logical development. At times the style almost achieves the effect of the interior monologue and stream of consciousness—and this a few decades ahead of Joyce.

Unfortunately, this use of the old style is not generally a happy choice for Futabatei. The very first phrase of the novel, for instance, "Chihayafuru kannazuki," means simply "October," for which the ordinary word is *jūgatsu* (tenth month). The epithet *Chihayafuru* is a vestigial formula-term (*makura kotoba;* "pillow word") from the ancient formulaic tradition; it means "who shakes the world with a thousand rocks (thunder and earthquakes)" and hence "powerful, strong"; it is always applied to deity. *Kannazuki* is an old term from the lunar calendar meaning "the *god*less month" (hence the epithet). This type of formulaic expression, together with puns, might of course intensify poetic ambiguity and irony, and William Empson probably would have approved of it. But after centuries of overuse such verbal techniques began to lose their appeal for the reader, and Meiji writers were by this time actively boycotting a convention they felt was functioning now as mere superficial ornamentation. For instance, Futabatei's readers would hardly pause at "earth-shaking godless-month" to consider a possible religious comment by the author on his "ant-like" crowd of modern bureaucrats; they would quickly gloss over the phrase as a quaint name for October.

Then there is the summer evening scene where Bunzō tries to talk to his flippant cousin, and a description of the moon is given:

> The cool moon rose, outlining the leaves of ten slim bamboo trees which stood in the corner of the garden. There

was not a single cloud and its powerful, radiant, white light lit up the face of the sky. Glistening drops of light poured down to the earth below. At first the bamboo fence between the houses held back the moonbeams and they extended only halfway across the garden. As the moon rose in the sky, the moonbeams crept up to the verandah and poured into the room. The water in the miniature garden there shimmered in the light; the windbell glittered and tinkled. Then the moonlight silhouetted the two young people and stole the brightness of the single lamp in the room. Finally it climbed up the wall. (P. 217)

An exquisite film fadeout. But the highly stylized and heavily Chinese texture is not related at all to the real movement of the characters' feelings. It appears that the elegant and archaic passage with its verse-like rhythm (5–7 meter) provides Futabatei with an escape from his job of scrutinizing the actual situation of that moment as it abruptly leaves the level of reality the novel has thus far been negotiating. The "beauty" and "elegance" of the passage do almost nothing to further the psychological drama between the young lovers. It is too easy a way out.

Another passage of this sort is the description of Ueno Park:

Fall in Ueno Park. Ancient pine trees stood row upon row, their branches interlaced, their needles thick and luxuriant, of a green so deep as to saturate the heart of an onlooker. The fruit trees were desolate in contrast; old and young alike covered with withered leaves. The lonely camellia bushes, their branches laden with flowers, seemed to yearn for companionship. Several of the delicate maple trees had turned a blazing red. The cries of the few remaining birds mirrored the sadness of the season. All at once, the wind blew sharply. The branches of the cherry trees shivered and trembled, shaking free their dead leaves. Fallen leaves strewn on the ground rose as if moved by a spirit and danced about in happy pursuit of one another. Then as if by unanimous accord they lay down again. This bleak and dreary autumn scene cannot compare with a bright and hopeful spring day, but still it had a special magic of its own. (P. 267)

"Branches interlaced," "a green so deep as to saturate the heart of an onlooker," "the lonely camellia bushes," "yearn for companionship"—phrases as cliché as the dance of dead leaves. Futabatei's painterliness is heavy-handed, even in the English. It is a set picture, almost that of a traditional scroll. Compare this with a passage from Turgenev's "The Tryst," which Futabatei translated about this time:

A slight breeze was faintly humming in the tree-tops. Wet with the rain, the copse in its inmost recesses was for ever changing as the sun shone or hid behind a cloud; at one moment it was all a radiance, as though suddenly everything were smiling in it; the slender stems of the thinly-growing birch-trees took all at once the soft lustre of white silk, the tiny leaves lying on the earth were on a sudden flecked and flaring with purplish gold, and the graceful stalks of the high, curly bracken, decked already in their autumn colour, the hue of an over-ripe grape, seemed interlacing in endless tangling crisscross before one's eyes; then suddenly again everything around was faintly bluish; the glaring tints died away instantaneously, the birch-trees stood all white and lustreless, white as fresh-fallen snow, before the cold rays of the winter sun have caressed it; and slily, stealthily there began drizzling and whispering through the wood the finest rain.[21]

For Turgenev, a tree is a tree, the actual physical existence of which is conveyed through the word. If meaning emerges from his words, it is grounded in the life of the trees. For Futabatei, in contrast, meaning is imposed by his verbal trees—words, or pictures, exist, but not trees. (Partly, this is due to Futabatei's lack of ease with outdoor scenes. His genius being in the dramatic presentation of men and women, whenever he has to describe a scene larger than a room, he escapes into the elegant style which offers the security of a stereotyped convention.)

The Drifting Clouds puts the conventions to occasional good use in its imagery, particularly animal imagery for expressing Bunzō's sexual frustration:

> Since Osei had come home to live, worms had been breeding inside poor, unsuspecting Bunzō's heart. At first they were very small and did not occupy enough space to give him trouble. But once they started actively crawling around, he felt as though he were peacefully departing from this world and entering a blissful paradise. . . . But all too soon the worms grew fat and powerful. By the time Bunzō had begun to suspect that he was infatuated with Osei, they were enormous and were crawling about, anxious to be mated. (P. 212)

The translator is surely in error regarding the plural "worms." Although Japanese nouns can be grammatically either singular or plural, the word here definitely means "the worm"—that is, the snake, the phallic being of Bunzō. In fact, there is a boldly explicit pun, *soitai no ja,* in the passage. The phase literally means "anxious to sleep together," but *-ja,* a nonsignifying verbal suffix, being a homophone with another *ja* that means "snake," the phrase can also mean "the snake that wants to sleep (with someone)." Similarly, there are many feminine symbols—*hamaguri* (clam) and *shijimi* (top shell), for instance—and, all told, a surprising number of fairly explicit sexual and scatological expressions.

Clouds of course are a major part of the book's imagery: the clouds in the sky and "to cloud" in the sense of "to obscure" both appear throughout the novel, reiterating its leitmotif. The reader will recall that Bunzō spends most of his time "upstairs," close to the clouds, and in any case quite cut off from the ground floor where most of the daily activities of life are conducted. The upstairs room, suggesting the paradox of claustrophobic one-room confinement and spatial and psychological indefiniteness, is a fit location for him. And the same sort of symbolic notation system operates in the names of the main characters, which all suggest representative qualities. The Oblomov-like hero is named Uchimi Bunzō, meaning "Inland Sea" and "third son of *Bun* (writing)."

The name can also indicate "introspectiveness" and "three letters" (or "three cultures"—Japanese, Chinese, and Western?). Honda Noboru, "main rice field" and "to rise," is a suitable name for an energetic upward mobile in modern Japan. The name of Bunzō's domineering aunt, Omasa, "to govern," is no surprise, while that of Osei, her charming, light-hearted daughter, means the "course of things," though it can also mean "force" and "vigor," which may suggest some untapped strength she inherited from her mother. Given all this, to read a point-by-point allegory of proper names may be overdoing it. We have to keep in mind that Futabatei knew his Dickens and Thackeray well, and must have learned from their not-so-subtle use of names as a prop to reinforce the orientation of a work.

But beyond this, the most important stylistic feature of the work is, of course, *gembun'itchi,* the kind of colloquialism that both Bimyō and Shōyō wished, but could not themselves begin to write. The quaint elegant style appears quite often in Part One, less frequently in Part Two, and hardly ever in Part Three. The time Futabatei spent working on the novel no doubt explains the change, but his own understanding is that the three parts, written at different periods, were modeled after different writers: Edo novelists for the the first part, Dostoevsky for the second, and Goncharov for the third.[22] But whatever the generic circumstances of the gradual disappearance of archaism in *The Drifting Clouds,* it should be noted that the later parts are much more serious in confronting the psychological movement of the characters. Anything that can be called an event in this "novel of no events" occurs in the earlier parts, and toward the end all the action takes place in the minds of Bunzō and Osei. Since the elegant style is linguistically alien to psychological drama, a totally new kind of colloquialism is called for. To twist it around, Dostoevsky and Goncharov—whom Futabatei discovered for Japan—taught him a style that called for a new subject matter. Serious study of an ordinary person's thought and behavior ultimately requires a language rooted in his ordinary life, and a novel written in such a language will of necessity have to deal with the daily life of the ordinary person. Despite Futabatei's occasional successful use of the quaint and unpunctuated style, his real achievement was in forging a plain, ordinary language to be used in the novel of plain, ordinary people.

With regard to the characters in *The Drifting Clouds*, Futabatei's best work is in dialogue and the main characters' self-analysis. He is also, however, adept at the swift presentation of minor characters. Both the old teacher and the department head who fires Bunzō are successful caricatures of the kind of "Westernized" men who have been crowding the Japanese literary scene ever since. Though self-convinced connoisseurs of the West, they in truth know very little of it, or of Japan either for that matter. While drawn with broad satiric strokes, these two characters also amplify certain traits shared to some degree by the younger characters—Bunzō, Osei, and Noboru. And they gloss a noticeable contradiction within Bunzō himself, who, though generally a sympathetic figure, self-righteously refuses to "apple-polish" his boss, at the same time doing exactly that to his old teacher. Using minor characters to gloss or amplify the traits of the major figures is a common enough technique in fiction but Futabatei's skillful use of it here gives us impressive and tangible evidence of his knowledge of such novelistic resources.

Omasa is a type character, and what a sardonic portrayal of powerful maternity she is. Utterly unself-conscious and seemingly indefatigable, she snorts and belches along, secreting her venom for her unfavorite people and then letting them have it. Similarly, Noboru, the vulgar but quite self-assured social climber, is very much alive. The verbal exchange between these two big-mouths is a comic masterpiece.

Where Bunzō is concerned, his extreme shyness and taciturnity make the author's good dialogue technique irrelevant. His thoughts must somehow be conveyed, but there is the problem of how to proceed. Since he vacillates so interminably, a third-person narrator's presentation and interpretation would be awkward and boring: how could any other person, particularly the narrator, be interested in his endless does-she-or-doesn't-she and should-I-or-shouldn't-I debate with himself? Bunzō had better speak for himself. He had better, but he doesn't. The novel is not told from the well-focused point of view of its chief character. In fact, the narrator maintains an ironic and rather condescending distance from the character, especially in the earlier parts. Here is his earliest description of Bunzō, for instance: "His complexion was quite poor, pasty and sallow, but his thick eyebrows lent distinction to his face, and the bridge of his nose was straight. His mouth was not very shapely but it was firm and restrained. He had a pointed chin and prominent cheekbones. He was rather drawn and seemed nervous and not particularly appealing." (P. 198.)* Even at the end of the novel, where Bunzō at long last reaches some sort of resolution, the narrator presents him ironically:

> Restlessly he wandered [back and forth in the corridor]. Eventually he reached a decision. He would try to talk to her when she came back. He would gamble everything on her response. If she would not listen, he would leave that house once and for all. He went back upstairs to wait. (P. 356)

Note his restless movement "back and forth" † in the house; also his final move in the novel, which is a return to his upstairs room, an ivory tower of sorts, protected from the context of life. If a novel can be said to judge events and characters, it must certainly be said of *The Drifting Clouds*.

Now, if the narrator seems ironic at both ends of the novel, it is logical to ask what the perspective of this irony might be. And how about other passages, especially in the later parts, where he seems so intensely involved in the hero? In Browning's dramatic monologue, the authorial stance is unambiguous in its irony and the character is made to reveal himself in spite of himself. It is the same in the omniscient-narrator novel: the narrator's comments add up to a definable commitment on the part of the author himself. But what is the narrator's judgment in *The Drifting Clouds*? What does his irony mean? Is this young man—painfully honest and credulous and finally quite ineffectual—an object of pity to the narrator? Or is he somehow praiseworthy as a kind of

---

* Do we see in this portrait a version of the entire Hamlet-Gothic villain-Byronic hero-Oblomov lineage? A very much tamed version, but it does betray something of Cain's mark.

† Ryan's phrase "wandered about" is imprecise. "To and fro" or "back and forth" would be more appropriate.

modern moralist? Or, still another possibility, is the narrator saying that he *is* modern man? And finally, is life "sad" or "gay" in
Futabatei's eyes? Is Bunzō tragic or comic? Or a little of each?

I do not believe we shall find a clear answer to these questions.
The Drifting Clouds, for all the hero's propensity to moral judgment, affords no perspective in which his broodings might take on
some significance. Melville's Bartleby, Goncharov's Oblomov,
Dickens's Eugene Wrayburne, for instance, all exist in a moral
and psychological context in which their paralysis is precisely defined; in Uchimi Bunzō we have a fragmented modern man portrayed without a clue to his broader significance. The narrator is
as unsure about Bunzō as Bunzō is about himself. It must be then
that the irony in the narrative voice originates in the author's
own feeling of fragmentation, his awareness of his inability to
organize a coherent judgment vis-à-vis his character.

Osei, pretty and faddish—a flapper, if such an anachronism
might be allowed—is similarly ambiguous. Often dismissed by
critics as a superficial "new" girl, she is actually extraordinarily
charming. She has a shallow sort of crudeness, true, but it is nev-
ertheless balanced by her refreshing temperament and free energy.
Osei also undergoes certain changes in the course of the novel.
From chapter 12 through chapter 16, she is no longer such a flirt,
but rather subdued toward Noboru and her cousin and attentive
to her mother. In a rare passage that directly squares with her
inner thoughts, there is even a moment of self-realization. But
what does it mean? What are we supposed to think of her now?
And how does Bunzō see her now? There is no direction coming
from the narrator here. To our frustration, he provides no clue to
such questions. Just as he was uncertain about his modern young
man's predicament in the loss of being, so is he now unsure of the
girl in the picture—this time, simply because he does not seem to
understand what a girl is. Potentially there is a full-bodied young
woman—lively, good-looking, affectionate, shallow, callous, sexy,
pretentious—but the narrator does not gather these features into
a sharp focus so we can see her clearly. We don't know what to
think of her any more than Bunzō does.

The novel is formed by one person's consciousness of another.
Each character's understanding of himself is modified by the

other's notion of him. And this interlocking of consciousnesses creates the world of the novel, the community of men and women as the novelist perceives it. What is curious about *The Drifting Clouds* is how little the characters seem to understand each other despite the fact that they are living in the same house, having their meals together, and sitting down in the evening together. Their physical world is one small house, and yet the residents are worlds apart, each one isolated with no promise whatever of better understanding in the future. Omasa and Noboru, vulgar-minded as they are, dismiss Bunzō too casually, and that ends the matter right there. Between Osei and Bunzō, there is little promise of any greater insight.

What we begin to suspect after a while is that Bunzō does not know Osei at all. Her sexual energy is obviously attractive to him, but Bunzō, Confucian puritan that he is, is afraid to think very well of sex, which is finally "wantonness," even "obscenity," as he unhesitatingly defines it in relation to his rival Noboru. The moral-psychological terms available to him are neither extensive nor sophisticated enough to apply to a modern young woman who owns her own mind, and, alas, her own body. Bunzō does not see Osei herself but his own restricted image of her, which is mere fantasy and illusion, and he knows it:

> Bunzō was certain that her new attitude toward him contained a significance that he was not yet able to grasp, and he was determined to find out what it was. With an enormous effort he concentrated all his energy on analyzing her behavior to isolate this evasive element. He had little success. He became irritated. And then those devilish worms inside him started their tantalizing dance again, teasing him with one hint after another, and finally tricking him into accepting some absolutely absurd solution. Half realizing how ridiculous it was, he accepted it for the moment anyhow and worked on the idea until he had constructed a whole situation from it. He experienced exactly the same hurt and pain from this artificial hypothesis as he would have if it had been a fact. At last he made himself see it for what it was: a ridiculous fantasy. He was

simply looking for trouble. In a rage of self-disgust, he mentally smashed the illusion into a million pieces. He sighed with relief. (P. 274)

And, finally, we suspect that the narrator—indeed the author—shares with his character much the same ambivalence, the same fogginess and irresoluteness. The astonishing lack of mutual understanding among the characters of *The Drifting Clouds* cannot be explained solely in terms of Osei's superficiality or Bunzō's obtuseness. Nor can the surprisingly complete separation of the characters be interpreted as a result of the paradoxical privacy prevailing in the apparently communal Japanese home. There is doubtless something here of Futabatei's personal isolation, which was nearly absolute in a real sense for many periods of his life.

One might connect this moral ambiguity with the technique of temporal obfuscation discussed earlier. *The Drifting Clouds* is a moral and psychological novel in the sense that the hero is possessed of a compelling moral sensibility, and the narrator obviously tries to deal with it. The hero's action must then be anchored in the chain of events arranged from a temporal-causal viewpoint. The novel is, however, quite vague in its temporality, and as a result the hero's action is suspended in its clouds of anxiety without being rooted in the context of everyday temporal sequence. The novel, in short, tries to judge the hero from a point of view, while it has no point of view. The narrative sequence, disrupting the temporal sequence, is both a symptom and a strategy of this frustrated judgmental effort.

The Drifting Clouds neither defines the nature of its own irony nor demonstrates much conviction that irony might turn out a saving grace in a world of grotesque absurdities. And yet it is an important modern work for the way it disdains the crowded panoramas that tease fiction into episodic surveys, and for the way it manages to transform behavior into motivation and action. Similarly, its language, while using the conventions to its advantage, pushes the frontier of the craft of fiction to the border of colloquialism.

Futabatei wrote two more novels after an interval of twenty years. *The Visage* (*Sono Omokage,* 1906) describes a married man's love for his wife's sister. The consummation of their love produces an awful guilt in the girl, and the man, a university lecturer, abandons family and career and disappears on the Continent to become eventually a skid-row alcoholic. Here again, the novel suspends judgment on the tormented man. Though the language is plainer, more in tune with other novels being written at the time (which had caught up with *gembun'itchi* by then), this novel lacks the attractive concentration of *The Drifting Clouds*. Futabatei's last work, *Mediocrity* (*Heibon*, 1908: translated into English in 1927), is quite boldly autobiographical. At the beginning of the *shi-shōsetsu* (I-novel), the orthodox tradition in the modern Japanese novel, *Mediocrity,* is interesting to a historian. But from the point of view of art it does not come up to *The Drifting Clouds.* For one thing, it peters out unpleasantly at the end, confirming a tendency already evident in the author's earliest work, [23] but not so damaging there.

Futabatei is one of the few really attractive men of Japan's modern literature. Honest to a fault, he refused to join the Tokyo literati, with their jealousies, petty backbiting, and continually compromised positions. He hated to think of himself as a writer, preferring the man of action as a self-image. In fact, to be true to himself he abandoned his writing career soon after *The Drifting Clouds,* and during the rest of his short life was in turn a journalist, a colonial administrator, and a teacher. Even in these capacities he refused to sell out, and no doubt as a consequence he never really succeeded in his ventures. Now, of course, his genius is recognized, and despite his meager production he is considered a giant among Japanese novelists.

II

THE IMPORTED LIFE

MORI ŌGAI: *The Wild Goose*
—*Japan is not a land of art.*

Mori Ōgai published his first fiction in 1890. To think of
"The Dancing Girl" (*Maihime*) as anything but juvenilia is hard
for most of us now, but Meiji readers found it otherwise: with the
exception of a very few critics, it was a perfect modern masterpiece for them.[1]

The language of "The Dancing Girl" is in a decorous elegant
style (*gabun-tai*), although contemporary readers took it as a
"mixed style of Japanese, Chinese, and Western" (*wa-kan-yō-
setchū-tai*), feeling that the scattering of German words and names
through the story was the most important stylistic feature. The
elegant style of "The Dancing Girl" reads well even today, being
neither too difficult to understand nor too familiar as the colloquial
style might be. The nostalgia created by the old-fashioned language matches the exotic setting and experience described by the
story, which was at least part of the reason for its instant acclaim.
But at this particular juncture what mainly interests us is the
hero's experience, which provides one of the earliest examples of
an attitude toward the West that has since grown into something
like a version of pastoral in modern Japanese fiction.

The story runs like this. A young career government worker,
assigned to a few years' study in Germany, meets a struggling

young ballerina in Berlin and saves her from a threatened seduction. He falls in love with her, and they live together, but this highly irregular behavior invites his superior's censure, and he is dismissed from his position. Down and out in a strange land, he struggles to survive on a few free-lance writing assignments for Tokyo newspapers. Then an old friend of his who happens to be in Berlin as secretary to a visiting official offers to help him on condition that he give up the girl and return to Japan. He accepts the offer. The girl, now pregnant, discovers his plan and suffers a breakdown. He goes home anyway, but on his return voyage he writes of his feelings of guilt and regret, and this first-person record constitutes the story.

In the earlier part, the young man thinks about the meaning of all the hard work that has put him through the highly competitive university system. Even his sojourn in Europe is part of this life-long program "to become a name, to raise his family's name." [2] Once in Germany, however, he begins to feel profoundly disturbed by his "passive and mechanical" personality. The freedom and independence that he breathes in the European air threatens to float him loose from the tight structure of his native society. Work now appears to him as a deception, of others as well as himself, the motive for work being only greed and the fear of ostracism. What he used to believe was great moral dedication to learning is no more than selfish and bureaucratic careerism.

At this point in his critique of self and society he meets his German dancer, with her "pale golden hair," "pure blue inquisitive eyes bedewed with tears," "long eyelashes," and, of course, "white skin." Clearly, she stands for the "freedom and independence" that are unattainable at home. The interracial aspect of the encounter—the relationship of the darker-skinned young man and the white girl, such as black writers have analyzed recently—is also unattainable except abroad and is a large element in the freedom he is experiencing.* But there is still something else in-

---

* One of the most interesting studies in this connection is an article by Hirakawa Sukehiro, "Fushinchū no Kuni Nippon: Mori Ōgai no Tampen to Lengyel no Jinshugeki *Taifū* o Megutte" ("Japan 'Under Construction': Mori Ōgai's Short Story and Lengyel's Race Drama *Typhoon*"), reprinted in the Nippon Bungaku Kenkyū Shiryō Kankō Kyōkai's collection of essays. According to Hirakawa,

volved. Although the German girl no doubt differs in appearance, in practically every other aspect she is conceived by Ōgai in the familiar terms of a Japanese girl. She is penniless and helpless, so the young man can take her in and be protective; she is "pure," "virginal," and, above all, faithful and devoted in taking care of her new lord and lover; in sum, she is not so much the pure Fräulein as the idealized Japanese wife and mother.†

There is nothing extraordinary about a writer's projecting his own ideal upon the people his hero encounters in a foreign setting. Indeed one could cite a long list of works including Melville's *Typee*, Charlotte Brontë's *Villette*, or, more contemporary to Ōgai, Henry James's European novels. But there are some specific features that should be mentioned in the case of the Japanese traveler-writer. And here we might look directly at the significance of foreign travel for the Meiji era Japanese.

Going abroad, or *yōkō*, was, at least until very recently, a glamorous affair in which the excitement of the event itself was combined with the promise of an élite career to follow. A young man's departure for such a grand tour constitutes a tribal occasion, with a great number of people properly seeing him off and wishing him well. The traveler carries the honor of the celebration with him sometimes, it is true, unduly burdened with a resolve not to let "expectations" down too much. He must test his foreign-language ability; he must know how to handle interracial encounters; he must try and prove his resilience of mind and person.

Melchior Lengyel's play *Typhoon* (1909), which treats a liaison between a Japanese student and a French woman in Paris, was so fascinating to Ōgai that he then translated one of the obscure Hungarian playwright's short stories. A racist work, *Typhoon* shrewdly exploits the European fear of the repressed and enigmatic Japanese. (Incidentally, many Japanese liked the play, which was produced at the Imperial Theatre in Tokyo in 1915.) Ōgai wrote two tracts on the subject of the Yellow Peril, very much in the air at that time, both of which dispassionately introduce the theories of white supremacy, refuting obvious distortions and contradictions. It is to his credit that there is no trace of the counteradvocacy of Japanese supremacy in either of these papers. ("Jinshu Tetsugaku Kōgai" and "Oka Ron Kōgai," *Complete Works*, XIX, 377–420, 421–66.)

† This impression is undoubtedly reinforced by the use of honorifics (*keigo*) necessitated by the Japanese. While he most probably could not have avoided it entirely, he might have done something to soften the tone of male dominance in the work, which even manifests itself in the pronouns.

Traveling, so seen, is a final test in the long apprenticeship to a secure position in the élite corps of the Empire. Still, the temporary release from the constraints of Japanese society is in itself a profound enough experience, more often a positive one than a negative. Instead of being held to a definite slot in a tightly meshed hierarchy, the traveler is cut loose to float free for a while in the unfamiliar medium. Even where he tends to cling to other Japanese tourists, compared to being at home he can move around almost unrestrictedly. If he is young and as yet unestablished, as is typically the case, he is likely to enjoy the freedom that goes with anonymity in a foreign city.

Then, there are of course the differences between his former Japanese life and that in which he now finds himself. Undoubtedly, comparison of cultures is a hazardous business, and the supposed vast differences between the East and West may or may not be bridgeable, or may indeed not even exist. But we are more concerned here with the felt contrast, not any absolute or objective difference, and the Japanese traveler is likely to see the West as the diametric opposite of the East, just as the antonyms imply. By him, the unfamiliar paradigms of Western life—respect for the assertion of individuality, the analytic habit of thought, the general tenets of democratic government—are felt to be the opposite of his native ones. Probably more important are certain matters closer to everyday living: fewer restrictions on the relations between men and women, more self-expressive manners and behavior, the colorful and luxurious appearance of European urban centers—so unlike what the young man had known at home. The tourist may at times react to these experiences with loneliness and alienation, but more often he will show relief and pleasure, even intoxication—until the time for starting home wakes him from his euphoria (as it did the young man of Ōgai's story).*

The re-entry shock upon coming home can cause long-term ad-

---

* The sociologist Nakane Chie presents the opposite view—the typical Japanese traveler as reluctant, homesick, and generally miserable—in her study of today's Japan, *Japanese Society* (Berkeley and Los Angeles: University of California Press, 1970), pp. 134–37. But Nakane is mostly interested in the businessman, for whom the encounter with the West is merely an inconvenient experience incidental to his main preoccupation with careerism.

justment problems. The same century lies there, but the traveler, now so accustomed to his role of observing as an outsider, a voyeur, is unable to reintegrate himself into the familiar become suddenly unfamiliar. He can't get his bearings quickly enough, and in any case he often finds the old scene unaccountably drab and stifling. Writers and intellectuals, even if their time abroad was miserable, as was Natsume Sōseki's, often suffer a particularly severe letdown.* The West has been inescapably internalized for these men in a way that can deprive their resumed life of the simplest pleasures.

To generalize boldly, modern Japan exhibits its contradictions most clearly to its returning émigrés: the country can no longer sustain the feudal fabric of community, but its corporate institutions insist on the bureaucratic loyalty of their vassals. The vertical relationship of parents and children is weakening rapidly, but more democratic family forms are yet to come. While the Empire expects its "subjects" to give homage to the Emperor, the wider world in various ways undermines nationalism as a source of intellectual and emotional satisfaction. Paternalism persists throughout society, cheek by jowl with rising "democratic" expectations. In short, while the old Japan is fast being secularized, the new myths tend to be stillborn.

"The Dancing Girl" is a convenient early index to this new East-West encounter which involves the fact and metaphor of traveling. But the story takes too easy a way out. When the young man finds "freedom" in Berlin, he is not really free. And when he really is free, alone with the girl, he is already crushed by the loneliness that freedom always brings in its train. Unlike

---

* See Ōgai's "Hidemaro stories," for instance. In "Fantasy" (*Mōsō*, 1911), Ōgai describes a certain fear he experienced before his return to Japan: "There is not the proper atmosphere to nurture the seed in the home to which I am now returning. At least not at present. I am afraid that the seed might die, having lived in vain. And I was assaulted by a fatalistic, dull, gloomy feeling." *Complete Works,* IV, 116.

Feelings of letdown are described by many other writers. One of the most typical examples is Yokomitsu Riichi's sprawling novel *Ryoshū*. The young men and women in the novel are continually haunted while in Paris by the idea of the return home, or, more specifically, frightened by the thought they might find themselves changed on their return.

Melville or Dickens or James, who use foreign experience for the projection of their personal vision, Ōgai is inescapably bonded to the vision he shares with the rest of his society. There is nothing "personal" about his Japanizing of the German dancer; it is as though the character—and the author—had not known the independence of the self at all. It never occurs to the young hero, for example, that it might be a real alternative for him to adopt Germany as his new home. Instead, he never doubts for a moment that his "foreign" experience will end sooner or later, and that what is possible in Germany cannot be in Japan. There is something fundamentally circular in his pilgrimage: he will stand at the end exactly where he stood when he started. His sojourn is a glorious moment of suspense to be treasured in memory perhaps, but finally irrelevant to his necessary being. Thus the hero's blaming his friend at the end of the story is an absurd self-deception. "The Dancing Girl," once hailed as Japan's earliest "romantic" tale,[3] unromantically insists throughout on maintaining safe ties to the work-oriented Japanese society, and thus stops far short of a serious examination of the choice between both work and freedom and social bondage and personal fulfillment.*

Ōgai wrote two more elegant-style stories, which, with "The Dancing Girl," form a European trilogy. Both highly successful at the time, they are very much the sort that had great vogue all over Europe in the early nineteenth century. Ōgai, it appears, made use of the exotic "gothic" setting, with its aristocrats and castles and mysterious deaths, to lure the Japanese reader to a land of enchantment far away.

---

*Ōgai wrote "The Dancing Girl," surprisingly enough, as an explanation of his own travel experience. A graduate of the Tokyo University Medical School, he joined the Imperial Army Medical Corps at twenty, and the army sent him to Germany two years later. We do not know what adventures he had in Berlin, but we do know that a German girl called "Elis" (also the ballerina's name in the story) followed him to Japan two weeks after his return. Ōgai refused to meet her, and through his family persuaded "Elis" to go back to Germany at once. "The Dancing Girl," written less than a year and a half later, is thus autobiographical and belongs in a way to the *shi-shōsetsu* tradition. This explanation, incidentally, was intended for his superiors in the army. Nothing is known, of course, about the story's effect in pacifying the misgivings of his inquisitive superior officers.

There are many stories, written much later, that fit better
thematically with "The Dancing Girl." For instance, "Under Reconstruction" (*Fushinchū,* 1910). A career civil servant reserves
a room in a restaurant undergoing noisy remodeling. While he
awaits the arrival of his guest, he notes the depressing mess the
room is in: "Japan," he reflects, "is not a land of art." * The
woman of the rendezvous finally arrives—a German soprano,
now on a world tour, with whom he was once involved during his
stay in Germany. As they fill in the gaps since the old days, she asks
him to kiss her. His answer, "We are in Japan," carries the crude
illogic that the kiss enjoyed in Dresden is not possible in Japan.
Reasserting the solution of "The Dancing Girl," though more
bluntly, the story reveals a slight tinge of sadness only in the
title ("Under Reconstruction"—everything held in abeyance until Japan itself is reconstructed) and the generally depressing
scene. The story is taut, with few details, but Ōgai's facile sentimentality manages to break through nonetheless. For instance:
"It was still only half past eight when a solitary, black car drove
slowly along the Ginza through an ocean of flickering lights. In
the back sat a woman, her face hidden by a veil." [4] The loneliness
would have been more convincingly *his* than hers. Besides, the
temporary wait implied by "under reconstruction" seems to hide
the depth and seriousness of East-West differences which Ōgai
obviously felt.

While "The Dancing Girl" and "Under Reconstruction" have
a measure of fictional autonomy, many other stories are very
nearly essays with little care taken for plot or character. For instance, the series built around an aristocratic repatriate (called
Hidemaro)—"As If" (*Kano yōni,* 1912), "Hiccup" (*Shakkuri,*
1912), "The Wisteria Arbor" (*Fujidana,* 1912), and "Hammer-
ing" (*Tsuchi Ikka,* 1913)—endlessly and rather shapelessly argue
the cultural and philosophical issues of the day as they strike the
character's (the author's?) fancy. Dozens and dozens of recondite
names are dropped, such as von Hartmann, Lange, Schleier-
macher, Strindberg, and Eucken, fairly choking the stories. I am

* In *Complete Works,* Volume III (see n. 2). The translation used here is Ivan
Morris's in his *Modern Japanese Stories* (Rutland, Vt., and Tokyo: Charles E.
Tuttle, 1962), pp. 35–44.

not at all sure these names meant anything much to anyone else at that time except the author, but those who admire Ōgai seem to take them at face value even now, as if the "stories" were important philosophical tracts. The most I can say for them is that they do reveal Ōgai's awareness of Japan's position vis-à-vis the West: Japan must "reconstruct" itself so that, presumably, it will ultimately "catch up with" the West (which, in this view, has already successfully solved most of the problems of modern life). "As If," for instance, questions the origin of the empire myth—precisely in the way that the nineteenth-century European Biblical criticism (say, Strauss and Feuerbach) questioned Christianity—and concludes tentatively that the myth should be treated *as if* it were history, all in order that Japan might eventually secularize the myth with the least pain as the West has done. Tentative accommodation seems to be Ōgai's strategy for most of life's predicaments.*

What *is* interesting throughout this is that Ōgai is no longer able —either in fiction or outside it—to talk about the problems of modern Japan without directly putting them in a Western frame of reference. Somehow an adequate explanation of one's experience requires a context provided by the West; or, more drastically, Japanese experience is somehow incomplete in itself. In order to become satisfying and significant, it asks for placement in a Western context where it can be viewed from a Western perspective. As the writer-hero of Ogai's thinly fictional novelette *The Youth (Seinen,* 1913) asks in his darker moments:

> Does a Japanese know at all how to live? As soon as he
> enters grade-school, he tries to dash through the entire
> period of schooling, believing there will be a life beyond
> school. Once he gets a job after graduation, he works year

* A brief look at Ōgai's later life is in order here. Concurrently with the spread of his fame as a writer, he steadily climbed the ladder of the Army medical services hierarchy, holding such positions as president of the Army School of Medicine, superintendent of army medicine, and surgeon-general of the Imperial Army—all at the highest military rank. Honored with doctorates both in medicine and letters, and with many medals and decorations, he is one of the very few Japanese writers to combine literary activities with a very successful establishment career. Yet his favorite motto in life was "Resignation," and as he was dying, in 1922, he is said to have mumbled, "Absurd."

after year until retirement, always thinking there will be
a life beyond work. But there is no life beyond. (*Complete
Works*, Vol. V, chap. 10.)

The young man never seems to find the proper subject matter for
his art: Japan is not interesting to him.

The importation of themes from the West is, then, a provisional
solution to the identity crisis in Japanese literature. Futabatei's
borrowing from Russian and Ōgai's from German are only two
cases out of a whole cultural process which for lack of a better
term must be called the "Westernization" of both art and life. To
clarify, we can force the argument a little. The "Westernization"
of a young man begins with his reading a European or American
novel. The pattern of behavior he finds there begins to loom in the
background of his own conduct. As he puts on jacket and trousers,
he feels "European." He kisses his girl friend, and he looks for a
Tolstoi heroine in her. He trims the Christmas tree (just one more
New Year's decoration), and begins to aspire to "Christian"
ethics. His external conduct affects his consciousness; but the
consciousness also modifies the conduct. At this point he can with
some legitimacy be depicted by a writer as living a "Westernized"
life in Japan, and the reader, too, can visualize himself as doing
the same. Nature indeed imitates art in Japan, and to a degree far
greater than Oscar Wilde could possibly have imagined. Along
with the methods and the products of Western industry and en-
gineering, many post-Meiji Japanese were eager to import not
just the West's literature and literary themes, but a new life-sub-
stance itself. And if all this looks like an insignificant ripple on the
surface of one's being, we must see that in a man's life no surface
change leaves the depths untroubled.

Ōgai's European studies continued, as can be seen in his trans-
lations from his characteristically wide range of authors—from
Rousseau, Goethe, Lermontov, Hoffmann, Andersen, Turgenev,
Daudet, Flaubert, D'Annunzio, Tolstoi, Gorky, Ibsen, Andreyev,
Strindberg, and Schnitzler to Shaw, Maeterlinck, and Rilke.* Dur-

---

* His translations are contained in 18 of the 53 volumes of the standard *Complete Works*. Although they are mostly from German and English, his range of
authors is indeed remarkable.

ing this time, he was also deeply absorbed in rediscovering the roots of his native culture. When, for instance, General Nogi, national hero and Ōgai's personal friend, followed the Emperor Meiji in death by taking his own life in 1912, in accordance with samural tradition, Ōgai's grief expressed itself in a series of semi-historical fictions treating the samurai code of *junshi* (joining the departed lord by suicide). His return to the past becomes even more dominant in the barely fictional and nonfictional historical studies written after *The Wild Goose* up until his death in 1922. And yet, it is as a reaction to the imported West, even as part of the Westernization program itself, that such a resurgence of Japanese themes ought to be considered, as I will try to show.

The Wild Goose (*Gan*, 1911–15)* was written precisely at the point in his work where Ōgai turned from Western to Japanese themes. Its subject matter is no longer the East-West encounter, and instead of civil servant and aristocratic repatriates its main characters are a coarse-grained moneylender and his naïve mistress. There is a handsome young medical student, but he is not particularly well versed in the lore of the West, and only at the end does he decide to go to Germany, thus joining the host of Ōgai émigrés. The novel then largely focuses on a style of petty-bourgeois life everywhere observable in Tokyo. Even the references the narrator makes to Tokyo stores, streets, and bridges and to the Edo entertainers are familiar ones for the reader and sketch a setting far from the usual Ōgai territory. For once, Ōgai seems to be writing fiction, as he digs out the life of ordinary Japanese in Japan. But is he really weaned from the West?

Suezō, once an errand boy, now runs a prosperous loan operation. He comes across a beautiful girl, Otama, just separated from a bigamous policeman, and wants her for his mistress. Suezō invites Otama and her father to discuss the proposal, and all agree to an arrangement: he buys a home for the girl and rents another for her father. Days go by, but Otama is too timid to go and see

---

* I use the English translation by Ochiai Kingo and Sanford Goldstein, *The Wild Geese* (Rutland, Vt., and Tokyo: Charles E. Tuttle, 1959). The plural form "geese" in the title is an error, since the title refers to the particular bird Okada kills toward the end of the story.

her father, fearing Suezō's possible disapproval. Soon everything
works out, and around Suezō's daily visits to Otama and her occasional visits to her father a semblance of peace prevails. Suezō's
jealous wife, however, hears about the liaison, and begins to nag
her husband. In the meantime Otama, who had been made to believe that her master was a respectable businessman, finds out
that he is actually a loan shark. To avoid worrying her aging
father she keeps the news to herself, which only increases her
sense of isolation. Just about this time, she begins to notice one of
the students who pass her house on their regular evening walks.
She learns his name, Okada, and his address. One day Okada
hears a commotion in front of Otama's house: a snake is swallow-
ing one of the linnets Suezō bought for her. Being the only man
around, Okada kills the snake and rescues the small bird. Otama
gratefully helps him wash his hands, but even then she is too shy
to speak to him. She knows by now that she is falling in love with
Okada, but sees no way to deepen their relationship. One day
when Suezō tells her that he will be away overnight, Otama
finally sees her chance and, giving her maid the day off, prepares
to invite Okada in when he passes by. This particular evening,
however, Okada is joined by his friend, who is the narrator of the
tale. Otama has no courage to speak to Okada in front of another
man, and they pass by. Okada tells his friend that he has been
offered a research job at the University of Leipzig and is leaving
Tokyo the next day. As they approach Shinobazu Pond, they are
joined by another friend, who suggests that Okada kill one of the
wild geese so he can cook it that evening. Half hoping that he will
just frighten the birds away, Okada pitches a stone and hits a
big one. As the three walk back with the dead bird, Otama stands
frozen in her doorway. "Her eyes, opened beautifully wide,
seemed to contain an infinite wistfulness and regret" (p. 118).[4]
The next day Okada leaves for Germany.

The narrative structure of *The Wild Goose* is a bit awkward,
a frequent problem with Japanese novels. The narrator, Okada's
friend, begins by reminiscing on past events, but soon disappears
from the tale, almost making it a third-person story. He returns
in chapter 18 when it becomes increasingly clumsy to present
events which the narrator cannot have been in a position to know.

His explanation of his knowledge is offered at the end—"I learned half the story during my close association with Okada [and] I learned the other half from Otama, with whom I accidentally became acquainted after Okada had left the country" (p. 119)— and is unpersuasive. (How could he, even with Otama's help, ever come to know the minds of Suezō and his wife?) Although the narrator resumes his role as a participating character toward the end, the occasional comments throughout the work are more authorial than first-person. In a way, the typical Japanese sentence form which allows omission of the subject (the verb having no inflection to indicate person or number) serves to reinforce this ambiguity around the narrator.

What might usually flaw a novel, however, is not altogether a weakness in this case. In the opening, the narrator's "I" is very prominent ("That date comes back to me so precisely because at the time I lodged in the Kamijō . . . and because my room was right next to that of the hero"). This implies that his relationship with Okada is more than just thematic. The "I" meets Okada as a self meets the other and becomes an observer of the other. Interestingly, the hero is himself a passive observer rather than an actor. Thus, as the voice shifts, confusing the hero's with the narrator's, the effect is to distance the events from the reader altogether. Similarly, the returning narrator's disavowal of involvement with the heroine at the end of the story—"It is unnecessary to say that I lack the requisites that would qualify me to be Otama's lover; still, let me warn my readers that it is best not to indulge in fruitless speculation" (p. 119)—further increases the irony, putting the reader outside the story to look at the goings-on from the perspective of an aloof observer.*

---

* In chap. 22, comparing himself with the hero, the narrator makes a curious remark about his own feelings for Otama (p. 109). The self-contradiction detectable in the statement ("I would have been happy if, like Okada, I had been loved by such a beauty" and "I would have gone so far as to stop at her house [and] love her as one loves a sister") is not an instance of authorial irony but poor artistic judgment on Ōgai's part. There are two circumstances one should be aware of in this connection. First, Ōgai knew only a certain kind of relationship with the women in his life. He used to call his second wife (having divorced his first) his "objet d'art." He seems to have been unable to engage himself at a close emotional level with women, and his relationships were all carried on as though from a dis-

The work explores several possible man-woman relationships in Tokyo life. To begin with Suezō, such an ambitious and energetic man cannot possibly be satisfied with an ugly woman like his wife, Otsune, who "press[es] on his stomach her heavy breasts, like pocket-warmers, which had supplied ample nourishment for each of their children" (p. 59).[5] As his store of wealth increases, his vitality seeks fresher outlets, although not to the extent of breaking up his marriage. With Otama, however, his sexuality does not seem as fully engaged as it ought to be under the circumstances. When he buys linnets for her, feeling "How charming [it is] to see her with them" (p. 83), he is utterly un-ironic. He really is in love with his bird-girl in a cage. No doubt he is happy in gently tutoring her, but the book clearly indicates their relationship will be short-lived. Sooner or later, Otama will have to fly from her cage. Thus does *The Wild Goose* coolly write off the shrewd moneylender's claim to fulfillment.

The narrator-author is plainly sympathetic toward Otama's growth from a gullible child "bride," to a beautiful young girl willing to sell herself for her father's comfort, and thence to a woman aware of her own need for happiness. This process of maturation is marked by several image notations along the way (of which the bird imagery is of course the most conspicuous). Here Ōgai avoids sentimentality rather well. Where necessary, Otama is portrayed as capable of shrewd scheming almost matching Suezō's. Not the "pure" nothing that wafts through so many Meiji novels (or their Victorian counterparts), she perfectly understands her sensual needs: "[Warm in bed after waking up] Otama would let her imagination go unbridled. Her eyes would glow, and the flush would spread from her eyelids to her cheeks as though she had drunk too much sake" (p. 101).[6] She must find the right man.

Her restlessness shows itself, just after she moves into her new

---

tance. Second, Otama was evidently modeled after a girl Ōgai himself saw occasionally, but only as Okada and the narrator saw Otama. In a more explicitly autobiographical, if rather parodic, story, "Vita Sexualis" (1909), the narrator-author presents a girl just like Otama. In the same way, *The Wild Goose* distances the author's personal experience by several removes through its narrative structure.

house, when she discovers Suezō's true status. A seemingly un-related incident occurs when a self-announced ex-convict invites himself into the house and forces money from Otama at *knife point*. Thus the intrusion of male sexuality into Otama's con-sciousness commences, and it is about this time that she begins to notice Okada. When the linnets are attacked, it is Okada who runs to the rescue, cutting the snake's head off—castrating him-self, and Suezō, too, at the same time. Thus this St. George, though reputedly a fine athlete and a connoisseur of Chinese erotic liter-ature, is neither a very virile lover, nor any substantial succor to anyone, linnet or girl.

Ōgai's almost too explicit handling of symbols culminates in Okada's killing of the wild goose. Otama's possibility of freedom is annihilated by this one, partly unintentional, act. Okada, the linnet's defender, has become the slayer of a goose, undergoing this change just as his involvement with Otama becomes a possi-bility. Clearly, she is left here with little but the prospect of frus-tration.

Accident plays too conspicuous a role toward the end. By acci-dent, Okada is not available for Otama's carefully arranged meet-ing; by accident, he hits the bird; and by unhappy coincidence, he is to leave for Germany next day. And yet, there is something much more stunning about the story in the way it—not Okada—kills off this "jewel of a girl" (a literal translation of her name). Despite the sympathetic treatment of her growth, the book thor-oughly extinguishes any hope she may have for the future when it quenches the possibility of Okada's becoming her lover. It is the same with all the other failed relationships—Suezō and his wife, Otama and her policeman "husband," Suezō and Otama, even Otama and her father—and by the end it is as though her story itself had been stoned to death like the wild goose. Of course, there are the two survivors, Okada and the narrator. But they, too, seem headed toward a dead end. As for Okada, whether he meets another ballerina in Germany or not, he will almost certainly have to come home again eventually, and then what? As to the narrator, he makes it plain to us that his life is a purely vicarious one. And so, with both appearing all too ready to join the other Ōgai

émigrés, we see that the Japanese setting has not after all engaged Ōgai as fully as he might have wished. There is no hope
at present for personal happiness in Japan.

But not having a happy life to live is not the same as having
no life to write about. In the very culture that Matthew Arnold
called "not interesting," Hawthorne and Melville were writing
their great novels.* And Otama's life, despite its desolate outlook,
does provide Ōgai with a subject matter to hang a story on. Yet
even here one recalls—as Ōgai's contemporaries must have—that
The Wild Goose was to some extent inspired by *The Wild Duck*
(1884), by Henrik Ibsen, whom Ōgai had been translating off and
on since 1903.† (Ōgai, by the way, is not responsible for the absurd
effect of the English title, "the wild goose"; the Japanese equivalents for the two titles, *nogamo* [duck] and *gan* [wild goose],
bear no such similarity.) It is not that the novel was modeled
on Ibsen's play, for the plot similarity is really very thin: the
friendship of Gregers and Hialmar; Hedvig's innocence and her
love for her father; Old Ekdal as a dependent father; Werle's
illegal business deals; Gina as Werle's mistress; such roughly
parallel circumstances do not add up to recognizable "sources"
for the Japanese tale. Besides, Ibsen's drama shows the master's
sure command of the form and his symbols weave thick layers of
meaning, whereas Ōgai's control of narrative form is often shaky
and his symbolism all too thin. Ibsen engages in the current pro-
lems of the culture in a way Ōgai does not. Still, despite all the
real differences between the two, the killing of the wild goose at
the end of Ōgai's work cannot be considered without reference to
the killing of the wild duck, which in fact turns into the murder
of the innocent girl Hedvig. The landscape of Shinobazu Pond

---

* *Civilization in the United States: First and Last Impressions of America*
(Boston, 1888), pp. 172–73. Of course, Arnold was not thinking particularly of the
novel but of the whole situation of American culture and there are vast differences
in circumstance between the two situations. Still there is some resemblance between
the cultural unsettledness of Meiji Japan and young America's lack of "culture" in
the nineteenth century. Also, one recalls that Hawthorne and Melville both wrote
"romances," which enabled them to transcend the restrictions of the culture with
a greater freedom than the strict "novel" would ever allow.

† He published translations of *Brand* in 1903, *Hedda Gabler* and *John Gabriel
Borkman* in 1909, *Ghosts* in 1911, and *A Doll's House* in 1913.

may have little in common with the Scandinavian parlor scenes of Ibsen's play, but the climactic emphases given the episodes in both works are remarkably similar in their effect.

A large inference is tempting here. Ōgai requires for his fiction a mode of experience that belongs to a foreign context of life. When he treats ordinary Japanese life, his creativity is not engaged: he either adheres too closely to actual life (as in his émigré cycle or his historical studies), or loses control and turns preposterous (as in the hero's relationship with an older woman in *The Youth*). In *The Wild Goose* the Suezō-wife-Otama relationship is stalemated, and Ōgai clearly had difficulty resolving it, as we can infer from the publication chronology. Chapters 1 through 21 were serialized between September 1911 and May 1913, but the intervals between installments gradually widened toward the end of this period. Then he was unable to continue at all for two years, until in May 1915 he added chapters 22 through 24 and published the whole work in book form. It is of course in these last three chapters that the killing of the wild goose takes place. In short, his worry over the ending of *The Wild Goose* did not abate until he developed the notion of the bird-killing and the exile of the hero.

The hero's departure for Germany is not just another plot detail. Only by taking him out of Japan and Japanese experience could Ōgai bring the story to its conclusion. Okada's further stay in Japan would surely have had to mean his involvement with Otama, and that would have required embedding the relationship in the Japanese context, thus reducing its significance and interest for Ōgai. Terminating the relationship by any other course of action on his part, such as going to another part of Japan, would have made him more active in deciding his role toward Otama, thus contradicting his essentially passive character, whereas the offer of the overseas job takes it out of his hands. Like the church bell in Victorian fiction, "going abroad" says something final and inevitable in the Meiji novel.

Ōgai was not alone with his problem. It may be that Japanese life was not yet amenable to the form of the novel as it is understood in Western literature. Possibly, the novel could not readily be born there at that time, as it could not in, say, seventeenth-century England. The novel needs a particular kind of life—a certain expectation or assumption—which Japanese culture, even today, does not easily make available. This necessary life withheld to greater or less degree, the modern Japanese writer seems to have two choices. He can fall back on his own personal life, which, having been lived, is factual and hence presumably plausible. The consequence of this choice is the tradition of the *shishōsetsu* (beginning around the time of *The Wild Goose*) which uses details of the writer's daily life, often at the expense of the work's form or even of his life's form, as we will see later on. Or he can invent, even fabricate if he will, a life outside the context of ordinary Japanese experience. Characters can be free and events extraordinary in any situation beyond everyday experience. Ōgai sends his characters abroad so that they may behave like the sojourners and outsiders they are for the moment. Of course, the foreign style can be found at times in Japan itself— among the aristocrats, for instance, about whom the bourgeoisie know very little. But then, the aristocratic class is itself a sort of Western colony, since its members are almost always expected to be more "Westernized" than the Japanese middle class, as we know from Ogai's "Hidemaro" stories and from Dazai and Mishima. Either way, abroad or at home, the introduction of Western life offers a solution for the problems that have arisen in the Japanese novel, itself an imported form. And it will continue to do so, until the imported life itself has truly taken root in Japan, making ordinary life a suitable substance for the novel.

III

THROUGH THE GLASS DARKLY

NATSUME SŌSEKI: *Pillow of Grass*
and *Light and Darkness*
—*What right have we to hope?*

When Lafcadio Hearn resigned from the University of Tokyo in 1903, his replacement, Natsume Sōseki, found it difficult to inherit even a small part of his great popularity. The literature students had especially loved to hear Hearn (known in Japan as Koizumi Yakumo) talk about Tennyson's poetry in his elegant yet informal style. Unlike Hearn, Sōseki was a Japanese, an obscure provincial college teacher no one had ever heard of, and his lectures were much too theoretical. Still worse, for students at the all-male university, he taught *Silas Marner*, a "high-school textbook by a woman writer." [1] Clearly, the new lecturer would never make it with the students. Fortunately, he was no longer convinced he had much of a vocation anyway, and after the great success of two novels he retired completely from teaching in 1907 and decided to live as a writer. Since he was quite famous by then, Sōseki's resignation was a newsworthy event, as was his refusal later to accept the doctorate conferred on him by the Ministry of Education, no other public figure having ever taken such an audacious action in those years.

Natsume Sōseki (1867–1916) had been a very serious teacher-scholar in English. Having first taught in Tokyo and in the provinces, he was sent to England by the Ministry of Education in 1900. With no more to spend than £15 (150 yen) a month, he lived an extremely frugal life—even by the foreign-student standards of recent years. He took the assignment altogether seriously. Not having luck like Ōgai's, he seldom ventured away from London, and spent his time shopping for books when he could spare the money, reading them, taking notes, and writing. He first attended W. P. Ker's lectures at the University of London; then, feeling the course was too elementary, he arranged for personal tutoring with W. J. Craig, the noted editor of the Arden Shakespeare. Having no way of meeting English scholars and writers, he found his intercourse with the English limited to nodding acquaintance with the lower-middle-class residents of his boardinghouse plus the few missionaries he had met on board ship. He never could sit down and talk to an Englishman who knew anything about literature or who could begin to guess some of the problems a Japanese scholar of English had to face. Craig, whose half-hearted tutorials cost Sōseki a precious seven shillings each, took him exactly as that, an extra source of shillings. Though pleasant enough, Craig was too much taken up with his own studies to take serious interest in the diminutive Oriental gentleman who came so punctually for his "lessons." [2] Thus Sōseki, it is safe to say, was considerably more miserable and less comfortable than most Japanese scholars who have come, apparently in very similar circumstances, in recent decades to the United States or England to study. His diary entries and letters of this time point less to his homesickness than to his bitterness toward England, a bitterness that he immediately directed back at himself for being a Japanese in the first place, especially a Japanese scholar of English literature.

> The two years I spent in London were the most unpleasant two years of my life. Among English gentlemen, I lived miserably like a lost dog in a pack of wolves. (Preface to *Theory of Literature,* in *Complete Works,* IX, 14; see note 2.)

> Everyone I see on the street is tall and good-looking. That,

first of all, intimidates me, embarrasses me. Sometimes I see an unusually short man, but he is still two inches taller than I am, as I compare his height with mine when we pass each other. Then I see a dwarf coming, a man with an unpleasant complexion—and he happens to be my own reflection in the shop window. I don't know how many times I have laughed at my own ugly appearance right in front of myself. Sometimes, I even watched my reflection that laughed as I laughed. And every time that happened, I was impressed by the appropriateness of the term "yellow race."

I was looking in a shop-window the other day when a couple of women passed by, commenting on the "least poor Chinese" [Sōseki's phrase]. I was more amused than angered by these expressions. . . . A few days ago I went out in a frock coat with top-hat, and a couple of working men sneered at me, saying "a handsome Jap." ("A Letter from London," ibid., XII, 36–37.)

If you want to be a scholar, you should choose a universal subject. English literature will be a thankless task: in Japan or in England, you'll never be able to hold up your head. It's a good lesson for a presumptuous man like me. Study physics. (Letter, September 12, 1901, ibid., XIV, 188.)

Talked with Brett. He said that the Japanese race needs improvement, and that intermarriage with Westerners should be encouraged for that purpose. (Diary, February 24, 1901, ibid., XIII, 43.)

We are country bumpkins, nincompoop monkeys, good-for-nothing ashen-colored impenetrable people. So it's natural the Westerners should despise us. Besides, they don't know Japan, nor are they interested in Japan. So even if we deserved their knowledge and respect, there would be no respect or love, as long as they have no time to know us and no eyes to see us. (Diary, about April 1901, ibid., XIII, 87.)

As time went on Sōseki became more and more isolated and depressed. But as though to fight off the despair, he was determined to read voluminously and continue working on a general theoretical ground for all literary studies. As we see from the theoretical studies—*Theory of Form in English Literature* (*Eibungaku Keishiki Ron*, 1903), *Theory of Literature* (*Bungaku Ron*, 1907), and *Literary Criticism* (*Bungaku Hyōron*, 1909)— for which the basis was laid during his stay in London, his orientation was of necessity toward justifying *his* English studies as compared with those of native scholars.

The *Theory of Form*, the first and shortest, discusses systematically what Sōseki proposes as the three areas of literary form. Here is the paradigm as he wrote it in English:

Form
> I. Arrangement of words as conveying the meaning.
>   (A) Form pleasant as satisfying intellectual demands.
>   (B) Form pleasant from various associations in a general way, outside of mere intellectual demands—Miscellaneous.
>   (C) Form chosen by our taste cultivated in historical development.
> II. Arrangement of words as conveying combinations of sounds.
> III. Arrangement of words as conveying combinations of shapes of words.[3]

Unfortunately, neither the principle of such a classification nor the contents of the categories can be easily understood, and the formula does not seem, finally, worth decoding. But what is clear and interesting to us is Sōseki's effort to classify, as for a taxonomy, all the "components" of literature, in order to know what territory he could appropriate as legitimately his in English without inviting the charge of intellectual deception. Like many such ambitious conceptions, his efforts at system building were bound to fail. We see how he necessarily falls short of an adequate definition of "universal literary form," which becomes a mysterious something that "appeals to our intellectual understanding in literature." One imagines he knew his shortcomings: the essay peters out to a shapeless conclusion despite the grand goal he sets for it. I am impressed nonetheless by the wide range of his references—from the classic figures to the major and many minor Romantic and Victorian writers. Moreover, Sōseki's analysis of a number of passages reveals an acute rhetorical sensitivity as well as his excellent historical command of the subject matter.

The second work, *Theory of Literature,* is the most ambitious of the three, with its objective of formulating the entire "content" of literary composition and response. According to some Japanese scholars, Théodule Armand Ribot provided the basic terms for this project, but Sōseki's framework, one suspects, being too singular to be anybody else's, is very much his own. Apparently believing that he has disposed of the problem of literary "form" in his first book, he now turns to the "content," which he divides broadly into two categories: "F" and "f." Large "F" stands for the intellectual focus of any content, and small "f" for its emotional overtones. I am, again, not at all sure how such a grand dualism can be expected adequately to explain complex literary processes, nor indeed am I clear as to what he means by literary "content." The titles of the sections seem to point vaguely to a general direction of argument: "Classification of Literary Content," "Quantitative Change in Literary Content," "Characteristics of Literary Content," "Mutual Relationships of Literary Content," "Collective F." Unhappily, by throwing every aspect of literature—from its materials, to rhetoric, to genres, to history, to grammar—into the "content" bag, he fails to make even the underlying assumptions of his system intelligible to the reader. And yet what impressed one about his first theoretical book is impressive here, too: his need to assess objectively the foreigner's claim to English literature, his continuous efforts to expand his own knowledge of English literary history, and, finally and very conspicuously, his sensitivity in actual analysis of passages and works.

The third work, *Literary Criticism,* is really a survey of eighteenth-century English literature. A belletristic history pure and simple, it yet again shows Sōseki's skill in close reading as well as his vast scholarship, his treatment of Pope and Swift being notably brilliant. That this book, the most historical and least theoretical of the three, achieves the most suggests that Sōseki's real gifts as a scholar lay in practical criticism where his sharp insights were backed up by his wide knowledge. At the same time, we should remember, Sōseki's theoretical objective was to prove that his studies were genuine and useful scholarly contributions. The sad part was that while his quasi-scientific theorizing failed to establish the possibility of a universal response—which, in transcending cultural and linguistic differences, might justify Sōseki's claim to scholarship in English literature, neither was there any good English critic around who could read his work in Japanese and tell him just how good—very good indeed—his practical criticism was. Thus in the Preface to *Literary Criticism* he seems to be conceding that a Japanese response to English literature cannot be significant to the English critic and reader, except in the way that the English historian's view of Japan is to the Japanese (naïve, interesting, exotic). While this is a kind of solution to his problem, his concession here thoroughly undermines the premise of his elaborate system: universality in literature.

Worries about the nature of literary scholarship were beginning to take form about this time. Within a decade or so, I. A. Richards and Kenneth Burke were publishing their attempts at rationalizing the discipline. And, a couple of generations later, academic critics the world over are again having their doubts about literary pursuits and the raison d'être of it all. Reflecting the unrest and discontent of their students, professors of literature are being forced to examine radically the ground of their work, if not their lives: a process leading them almost inevitably to the meanings of "relevance" on the one hand and "objectivity" on the other. For the Japanese professor of any European literature, however, such doubts are even more intense. He has the same fundamental uncertainty about his discipline, but on top of that is the nagging doubt about his personal authority as a professor of a literature completely foreign to his own. He may think he understands English, but what does "understanding" mean? How does he know whether he understands or not? Until recently at least, Japanese scholars have somehow managed to survive by repressing the basic problem and resignedly limiting their work to translating and annotating European works as "accurately" as possible. For the conscientious Sōseki, however, such worries could never be ignored while he continued to teach. Since he was never to gain much confidence in this work, he became increasingly depressed, until he found it almost unbearable to have to prepare his lectures and face his students. He disliked his colleagues, too, who at that time were beginning to emerge—there as elsewhere—as efficient and pretentious bureaucrats of learning. Thus, as his creative energy began to assert itself, he resigned from the university and became a staff novelist for the *Asahi* daily newspaper in 1907. He was to devote the rest of his short life— he died in 1916—to fiction writing.

It is perhaps significant that evidence for the theoretical basis of Sōseki's understanding of English literature should be so prominent in his own "Japanese" fiction. It is not merely that his works are full of the ironic spirit of Jane Austen, George Meredith, and Henry James, all of whom he loved. Rather, I am certain, the very form and substance of his fiction would not have materialized had he not been possessed of that rich and deep feeling for English fiction. The technique of the English novel which he knew and taught palpably shapes his own fiction and, furthermore, his knowledge of the English language works at crucial points in helping him forge a new language for the Japanese novel at this still early stage in its development.*

Before his university resignation, Sōseki published two novels, *I Am a Cat* (*Wagahai wa Neko dearu,* 1905–6) and *Little Master* (*Botchan,* 1906), and several short pieces, including essays on his visits to the Tower of London and the Carlyle museum and an adaptation of Tennyson's *Idylls of the King. I Am a Cat,* serialized very much like Dickens's *Pickwick Papers,* is a loose, open-

---

* I am of course not arguing that Sōseki's knowledge of English literature was his only inspiration here. As one can immediately discover, he read extensively in Chinese and Japanese literature as well. His friendship with Masaoka Shiki, one of the most important Meiji *haiku* poets, is also highly significant in his literary career.

ended satire which is surprisingly dark in places. The narrator is a stray cat adopted by a schoolteacher. Although this novel is at times too broad and transparent a caricature, its social milieu —that of ineffectual intellectuals and dilettantes surrounded by unsympathetic money-oriented bourgeoises—constitutes one of Sō-seki's lifelong preoccupations. His next work, *Little Master,* is a first-person record of an innocent young mathematics teacher encountering older and more experienced professionals in a provincial high school. The comedy here is even broader than in *I Am a Cat,* and while it reads with a refreshing pace and vigor, I miss the customary subtlety of Sōseki's satire.

Pillow of Grass (Kusamakura, 1906)[4] was written in a great spurt of energy and completed in just a week. It is by no means a "novel" in the usual sense, since Sōseki is boldly experimental here, as he will be for the next few years, producing a Bulwer-like melodrama, *Wild Poppy (Gubijinsō,* 1907), and the Kafkaesque *Miner (Kōfu,* 1908) before stabilizing his novelistic style, beginning with the trilogy of *Sanshiro, And Then,* and *The Gate* between 1908 and 1910.

The narrator of *Pillow of Grass* is a Tokyo poet-painter, well versed in both Oriental and Western arts and literature, who escapes the bustle of big-city life by visiting a remote hot-spring resort. Paralleling this movement, the work, which Sōseki calls his *"haiku* novel," [5] itself provides a tour out of "real life." There is little in the way of a story line: the "I" arrives at Nakoi, meets Nami, the eccentric and beautiful divorcée, and also gets to know her family, the Shiodas, and their friend, a Zen priest. At one point he witnesses the encounter of Nami and her former husband, and at the end he sees off Nami's cousin bound for military service in Manchuria. With so slight a plot, most of the significant "events" of the story take place in the narrator's mind, making *Pillow of Grass* a semi-diary account of an artist's moods and reflections.

> Going up a mountain track, I fell to thinking.
> Approach everything rationally, and you become harsh.
> Pole along in the stream of emotions, and you will be

swept away by the current. Give free rein to your desires, and you become uncomfortably confined. It is not a very agreeable place to live, this world of ours.

When the unpleasantness increases, you want to draw yourself up to some place where life is easier. It is just at the point when you first realise that life will be no more agreeable no matter what heights you may attain, that a poem may be given birth, or a picture created.

The creation of this world is the work of neither god nor devil, but of the ordinary people around us; those who live opposite, and those next door, drifting here and there about their daily business. You may think this world created by ordinary people a horrible place in which to live, but where else is there? Even if there is somewhere else to go, it can only be a "non-human" realm, and who knows but that such a world may not be even more hateful than this? (P. 12)*

The reader of the Japanese text is struck, first, by the wide use of the present tense and the prose cadence sustained by the extremely ornate diction, and after that, by a certain paradoxical feature in almost every statement. Although both of the English translations render the greater part of the book in the conventional narrative past, the original, like the quoted passage, is in the present tense throughout. Thus, while most novels move along a flow of time defined by the temporal sequences and consequences, *Pillow of Grass* progresses along a line of accumulated present moments. It remembers the past, of course, and it imagines the future.† And yet it constructs no novelistic perspec-

---

* All quotations are from the translation by Turney (see note 4).

† The most interesting way Sōseki indicates time in the novel is by his liberal use of the notions of East and West. Throughout *Pillow of Grass,* both Eastern and Western poets and artists are mentioned frequently, and generalizations drawn from the instances. According to the narrator, the East seems to represent an attitude that somehow transcends everyday matters—the "non-human" aspect of life—while the West suggests a down-to-earth involvement. (See his numerous comments on Shelley, Faust, and Hamlet versus Wang Wei, Tao Yuan-ming, and so on, as against his viewing the Western novel as "emotional," "intellectual," "social," "moral," "rational," "analytical.") Clearly, the correctness of his generalizations does not matter, for what Sōseki is trying to do is, first, locate the "non-human"

tive that can look back at a past incident or experience and place it in the plot. Things happen, and the narrator reflects on them as they are happening, but he does not know, as the novelistic (that is, past-tense) narrator usually does, where things will turn next. In such a story line the reader, of course, gets no ready-made interpretation and must puzzle and grope—as the narrator, too, appears to have to do—for a perspective that will make a "meaning" out of the story. There is an immediacy, even a certain excitement, in this for the reader, who is forced to pay attention to things as they happen or lose the thread.

The ornate diction is lost in the translation to English. But the Japanese version, too, has problems for its readers in its considerable number of Chinese ideograms that are both quaint and obscure. Although most Japanese can manage to approximate their meaning when they see them printed (on the basis of the components and, of course, the context of the ideograms), very few recognize them on hearing them. It follows that very few speakers of Japanese would know how to pronounce these obsure ideograms without the aid of *kana* notations,[6] even when they can guess the meaning. Such ideograms have effectively dropped out of the spoken language and may never in fact have been part of it. What this comes to is that Sōseki's writing in *Pillow of Grass* is, quite literally, far more visual than auditory; certain passages must be *seen*, not *heard*, to be understood. It is not accidental that the narrator is a painter. The very shape of an ideogram can suggest powerfully the shape and form of both a highly developed abstract concept and the vaguest sort of precognition.[7] This is not to deny the pleasant sonority of this passage in particular and the book as a whole—quite the contrary. But it appears to serve a purpose other than the pure euphony of the prose. The sound, in this view, is a useful propellant of the narrative line. Without it, we would pause too often in our reading and be tempted to parcel out the narrative time into a series of timeless scapes. In other

tour in the context of the world, and, second, to identify the roots of his imagination in the Eastern tradition. To treat the East as though it were exemplified by the spirit of Nakoi village is to look at the city, say Tokyo, as Western. The East is tradition and the past, the West the future. His sojourn in Latmos is then also a return to the past.

words, the cadence carries the reader along and occasionally makes him forget the untemporal, or spatial, features of *Pillow of Grass* that would otherwise distract and hold up his progress.

Paradox is the narrator's modus operandi in argument. At the outset, he divides man's faculties into intellect, emotion, and will, all of which he at once finds to be closed options. Life is disagreeable no matter what. Escape is necessary, except that there is no other life to turn to. Poetry and art, he argues, are born from this realization of having no choice. Quite early the narrator locates art (loosely including all the arts—literature, music, sculpture, and so on) outside the pale of the day-to-day human intercourse that leads only to the inescapable bog of paradox. Art is then what survives and transcends our disagreeable life.

The second cycle of this dialectic, reversing the order, begins on the next page. The narrator tells us that at twenty he thought life worth living; at twenty-five he found it paradoxical; and now at thirty, he seems to say, he finds ambivalence in everything— both joy and sorrow, health and pain, money and financial worries, love and fatigue. And how to resolve such an on-the-one-hand, on-the-other dilemma? The rock he slips on at this point, like Dr. Johnson's, stems his stream of thought and opens new possibilities. For a time, at least, the poet-painter stops worrying life into ever extending paradox and just sits and looks.

But the mode of progress throughout the work stays essentially the same: acceptance of life, its analysis into paradox, a new experience shifting the perspective of argument. When Sōseki called it a "*haiku* novel," he was thinking of a narrative movement determined by the juxtaposition and reversal of short scenes or thought sequences.

The movement of the argument is reinforced by the narrator's actual and metaphorical journey—from Tokyo and his "real-life" involvement with noise and paradox to an obscure mountain village and an aesthetic experience of uninvolvement. The poet-painter is determined to see the life he encounters in Nakoi as if it were "part of the action of a *noh* play" or, variously, to think of people as "moving about in a picture" (p. 23). He will keep his distance and irony in relation to life there: the "non-human tour" will be an exercise in disengagement.

Thematically, it is a familiar story. The English Romantics and post-Romantic writers Sōseki quotes in *Pillow of Grass*—from Shelley to Wilde—have argued time and time again: art needs distance from life, and at times almost supplants life to become a truer reality. Like Latmos in Keats's *Endymion*, Nakoi will give the protagonist a glimpse of Ideal Beauty. (The ideograms for "Nami" mean "that beauty.") To grasp it, however, the artist must first forego life. Although this position is almost always reversed at the end—as it is in *Pillow of Grass*, too—with the disinterested artist turning back into the thick of paradox, at the beginning at least, distancing to the point of alienation is the sine qua non of modern art. So much for the bare thematic restatement of what is clearly a very intricate narrative form designed to bring the reader along into the same perspective that the narrator takes for himself. His assumed aloofness toward Nakoi, the place and its people, is reflected remarkably in his verbal stance, as he proceeds to present Nakoi in almost purely visual terms, and the reader, too, begins to *see* the place as if it were a painting. Take, for instance, the scene of the tea-house in the spring rain; or the painter's dreamlike encounter with the Nagara maiden. There are also Nami's two histrionic performances—one in the bridal gown, the other with a dagger; the misty bathroom scene; Nami's rendezvous with her former husband; the Mirror Pond with the bloody red camellias; the final train-station scene. And every one of them a nineteenth-century topical painting—very "realistic," Pre-Raphaelite—translated into language, it is true, but altogether visual in effect. In fact, the scenes do not even refer so much to actual people and places as to certain already ordered visual forms. What is more, these self-contained stills are often extended into further metaphors and similes that are also visual and painterly. The pack-horse driver melts away in the fog "like some figure on a flickering magic lantern screen" (p. 25); the tea-house woman looks like a figure out of *Takasago*, a *noh* play, which in turn is said to look like a "tableau vivant" (p. 28).[8]

That a painter should see the world though a painter's eyes appears quite natural. But Sōseki's maneuver here is not for achieving an ever closer mimetic representation, but for creating a literary form that will more fully and more immediately involve his reader, who will thus be enabled to *see* the painting that Nakoi is for the painter. An essentially temporal art, the novel, is being maximally spatialized here. (One might recall here my earlier remarks about the visual feature of Chinese ideograms.) Instead of following a temporal evolution as the drama of the work unfolds, we are shown a series of discontinuous frames, with the effect of an ever changing perspective and the promise of a fresh, surprising perception with each new frame.

Take, as a good example of this, the way Sōseki introduces us to the heroine. The narrator hears about her from a conversation between the tea-house woman and the pack-horse driver in which they refer to her wedding. The painter pictures to himself the bridal procession and expresses it in a *haiku,* which then turns into an image of Millais's drowned Ophelia. (The Pre-Raphaelite Ophelia floating down the stream is a central image in the work, "floating" and "drowning" being its two important leitmotifs.) Meanwhile, the tea-house woman proceeds to compare the Shioda girl to the legendary maiden of the ancient *Man'yōshū* anthology who centuries before drowned herself, being unable to choose between suitors. Here is, then, the ever expanding (living) series of images—some gossip, a *haiku* image, an oil painting, a *Man'yōshū* poem; each one is taken up at a different angle and from a different context, a different tradition. And the metamorphosis in imagery continues after the poet-painter arrives at the inn: he dreams of the legendary maiden in a bridal gown, looking like Millais's Ophelia. The mixture of old Japanese poetry and art with Shakespearean drama and Pre-Raphaelite art almost crowds out the appearance of the actual girl we are about to meet. But there is even further amplification. Wakeful into the night, he keeps seeing a shadowy figure flitting about in the moonlit garden, and he tries again to arrest the vision in a series of *haiku.* He has a brief, very casual contact with the girl next morning, but the real meeting with this peculiarly elusive yet ever present girl comes much later, and that meeting *is* the whole extension of *Pillow of Grass.*

As the artist comes to know her better, Nami continues to appear from all sorts of unexpected angles: as a dancer-performer, a sharp wit, an eccentric. Her montage, too, becomes more complex: besides the Shakespearean Ophelia, the Pre-Raphaelite Ophelia, and the legendary maiden, we now have her own ancestor who drowned herself, and the generations of crazy women in her family. As each adds her own peculiarities to the composite, Nami takes on more and more the aspects of a generalized woman figure without at all losing her vitality and unpredictability.

The bathroom scene provides in a way the synecdoche of this process of knowing her.

> Leaning my head back against the side of the tank, I let my weightless body rise up through the hot water to the point of least resistance. As I did so I felt my soul to be floating like a jelly-fish. The world is an easy place to live in when you feel like this. You throw off the shackles of common sense, and break through the bars of desire and physical attachment. Lying in the hot water, you allow it to do with you as it likes, and become absorbed into it. The more freely you are able to float, the easier life becomes, until if your very soul floats, you will be in a state more blessed than had you become a disciple of Christ. Following this train of thought, even the idea of drowning is not without a certain refinement and elegance. I believe it was Swinburne who, in one or other of his poems, described a drowned woman's feeling of joy at having attained eternal peace. Looked at in this light, Millais' 'Ophelia,' which has always had a disturbing effect on me, becomes a thing of considerable beauty. (P. 102)

The sensation of floating recalls to him again the painting of Ophelia, which he now realizes attracts him because it epitomizes the notion of detachment, a loosening of the self and an abandonment to the flow of the water. It is as though he also has in the back of his mind some recall of the Edo *ukiyo* (floating world) tradition, for he now remembers his childhood experience of listening to a neighborhood girl practicing *nagauta*, the traditional Edo period *samisen* music.

Deep into memory though he is, he becomes aware of someone's approach. He account moves very slowly:

The dark shape descended to the next step without a sound, making it seem that the stone underfoot was as soft as velvet. Indeed, anyone judging from the sound would have been excused for thinking that there had been no movement at all. The shimmering outline had now become a little more clearly discernible. Being an artist, I have an unusually good sense of perception concerning the structure of the human body, and no sooner had this unknown person moved down a step than I realized that I was alone in the bathroom with a woman.

I was still floating there, trying to decide whether or not to give any indication of having seen her, when quite suddenly and without any reserve she appeared directly before me. She stood there surrounded by swirling eddies of mist into which the gentle light suffused a rose-tinted warmth, and the sight of her lithe and upright figure, crowned with billowing clouds of jet-black hair, drove all thoughts of good manners, civility and propriety out of my head. My whole being was filled with the realisation that I had discovered a beautiful artistic subject. (Pp. 105–6)

From disinvolvement to an instant of half-embarrassed interest to recovery, almost reflexively, of his customary aesthetic response to life. Continually emphasizing the need for distance between body and viewer, he recapitulates in the manner of an art historian the whole development of nude representation from Greek sculpture to modern French painting. Although the woman is at first only dimly visible through the thick steam, her shape becomes clearer moment by moment, until—the ornate diction almost suspending narrative movement—we are viewing an opalescent painting of Nami's body. Do we see her clearly? It is a case of now-we-see-her, now-we-don't, for just as he, and we, are about to close the distance and see her face to face,

Just then, however, her thick blue-black hair streamed around her with a swish like the tail of some gigantic legendary turtle cleaving through the waves. Next moment her white figure was flying up the steps tearing through

the veils of mist. A clear peal of feminine laughter rang
out in the corridor and gradually echoed away into the
distance, leaving the bathroom quiet again. The water
washed over my face, so I stood up. As I did so, startled
waves lapped against my chest, and splashed noisily over
the sides of the tank. (Pp. 108-9)

The narrative movement is as unexpected as a *haiku* reversal.
Electrically, still art is transformed into swift drama. Also, only
for an instant. For, just as his distance from the picture shrinks
and the possibility for dramatic involvement emerges, the actress
flies away, leaving the by now partly aroused narrator without
any participant. Irony, it seems, is built into the narrative movement itself.

The discontinuous story-line of *Pillow of Grass*—call it *noh*-
like, or *haiku*-like—is made fun of in one passage where Nami and
the artist talk about a Western novel (Meredith's *Beauchamp's
Career*, although not identified in the book):

"And because I am an artist I find any passage of a
novel interesting even when it is out of context. I find it
interesting talking to you—so much so in fact that I'd like
to talk to you every day while I'm here. I'll even fall in
love with you if you like; that would be particularly interesting. But however deeply I were to fall in love with you
it would not mean that we had to get married. If you think
that marriage is the logical conclusion to falling in love,
then it becomes necessary to read novels through from
beginning to end."

"What an inhuman way of falling in love you artists
have."

"Not '*in*human'; *non*-human. It is because we read novels with this same non-human approach that we don't care
about the plot. For us it is interesting to flip open the book
as impartially as if we were drawing a sacred lot, and to
read aimlessly at wherever it falls open." (P. 124)

If you think love leads to marriage, you must read novels from
beginning to end. The logic of *Pillow of Grass* is its converse:

love does not lead to marriage, and therefore novels do not need to be read sequentially. Only breaking the chain of causality will make life agreeable. And the thrust of this argument is reinforced by the way the intricate relationship of theme and form is woven. While the characters talk about making random dips into the novelistic reading sequence, *Pillow of Grass* is itself discontinuous, dip-into-able. Like two mirrors facing each other, the material of the novel reflects and amplifies the ironic dimension of the telling.

Perhaps the most fundamental irony of *Pillow of Grass* depends on the notion of detached art, or, to use its own term, "nonhuman" art. Nami, the Ideal Beauty, who like *Endymion's* Phoebe continually appears in a new phase, lacks something in her expression, despite the painter's repeated attempts to arrest her image in a picture. For the poet-painter, the best understanding of her comes, naturally enough, from seeing her as a remarkable pictorial subject. He is forever searching for that something required to complete *the* picture of the attractive girl. His final meeting comes about when he discovers for the first time an expression, never shown before, of what she may have been all along. He knows Nami's aloofness to her former husband, now impoverished and ready to leave the country; he also knows her bitter indifference to the fate of her cousin, who may die anytime on the battlefield. But in the last scene, where time and life reassert themselves in a crescendo through the symbols of river and train (very much as in Dickens' *Dombey and Son*), Nami betrays an emotion that is all too human. The painter at once realizes that the missing element all along was this "compassion." The picture of his Ideal Beauty is finished at last through his meeting with the real Nami. The Latmos of *Pillow of Grass* is not all that far from the call of life; the ideal picture a "non-human" art can produce must finally be utterly human. We see now that his notion of art— detached and uninvolved, "non-human"—must be radically modified. Art does not remain self-contained outside human intercourse. Beauty requires compassion; art needs humanity.

Just as it is about to close, *Pillow of Grass* thus opens up a new perspective. I see it as quite fitting that the novel should be so open-ended instead of completing itself as a self-enclosed art-form. A work that can begin anyplace can begin at the end. Sōseki is right: *Pillow of Grass* is indeed very much like a *haiku*.

There are ten years between *Pillow of Grass* and *Light and Darkness,* a decade in which European novels were being translated and published in great numbers along with much new Japanese fiction written in more traditional styles. Ideologies, too, ranging from nationalism to Marxism, were sprouting vigorously. The Japanese literary scene then, as now, strongly resembled the national political scene, with factions and schools centered around favored leaders, and with a kind of loyalty developing between master and disciples much like the feudal relationship of lord and retainers. In such an atmosphere literary theories tend to be less substantial than the vehemence of the adherents' convictions might suggest. The dominant literary school, for instance, was that of the "Naturalists," having as their spokesmen writers like Tayama Katai (1871–1930), Shimazaki Tōson (1872–1934), Kunikida Doppo (1871–1908), Tokuda Shūsei (1871–1943), and Masamune Hakuchō (1879–1962). But their actual works are far from "naturalistic" as we understand the term. Although they professed a debt to Zola and Maupassant, the influence is apparent only in their subject matter, which is usually restricted to the shady side of life. Otherwise, their techniques and assumptions are about as conventional and moralistic as those of any other group of writers at the time. Tayama Katai's *The Quilt* (*Futon,* 1907), commonly considered the best example of Naturalism, is the story of a middle-aged writer's suppressed love for his beautiful disciple. The most famous scene, almost embarrassing to read nowadays, occurs at the end where the hero buries his face in the girl's bedding after she leaves him for a younger man. But the story was shocking enough to Meiji readers, and it was at once ranked with *Germinal* and *Une Vie.*

The "Naturalism" of these writers consists then of little more than their misuse of the imported term, and before long in fact their manifestos pretty much disappear from the literary scene. There is one feature of their works that stands out, and that is their markedly personal and confessional quality. Soon to develop into a genre called *shi-shōsetsu* (I-novel), these works require that literature be "truthful." To simplify a bit, telling the truth here means: one, accuracy in recording; two, honesty in disclosure; and three, sincerity in confession. According to this recipe, the writer, in recording his own life, must present it in the worst light possible, but to do this, he must first have a "disreputable" life to write about—something of a problem, given the typical puritanic restrictions of Japanese life. Thus the adventures of these "bohemians" are pretty tame stuff, confined for the most part to the purchase of a willing lady for an evening. The rebels' politics, too, are disappointingly sedate, being largely apolitical and tacitly accepting the established social hierarchy of the Empire. Except for the few truly proletarian novelists who were able to survive the repression by the militarist regime around the 1930s, very few radicals were ever heard from throughout this whole period. In sum, the rebels' outrage is not outrageous, and their "accurate" recounting of aseptic political mischief and sexual misdemeanors (daily budgets and wife-beatings recorded as though of monumental importance) rapidly approaches the tedious.

The I-novel, nurtured in this stern tradition of absolute sincerity, however picayune it may become, banishes fiction as outright deception. Unfortunately, in the process it foregoes art as well. And Apollo is a vengeful god all over the world. For the primary task of the artist becomes, then, not exploration of good and evil in the framework of fiction, but the raw experiencing of them. The writer must now live the very substance of his work. The I-novel, in short, is essentially less a discipline in verbal craft than a "discipline" in lifemanship, an effort toward the achievement of a poetic life style.

Despite the early demise of "Naturalism" per se, the credo of confessionalism dies hard. In fact, it is the one most conspicuous characteristic of modern Japanese fiction as a whole, whether we are talking about Shiga Naoya or Dazai Osamu or Akutagawa Ryūnosuke or Nagai Kafū. And this abandonment of art and fictionality, the sine qua non of the novel, is one of the reasons so many of these same Japanese writers are almost unreadable to Western readers.

Mori Ōgai and Natsume Sōseki were the "anti-Naturalists" of

their time, both being strongly against fiction's abandonment of fictionality. While it is true that "accuracy" was important to Ōgai in his historical semi-fictions, he thoroughly parodied sexual confessionalism in *Vita Sexualis* (1909). And Sōseki, too, gave in somewhat to the naturalistic pressures in providing most of his novels with settings close to everyday life, and, in *Grass on the Wayside,* by following his own personal life in outward detail. Still, throughout Sōseki's works, there is much evidence of a critical awareness carefully sifting personal experience, so that even in *Grass on the Wayside,* his most autobiographical novel, the self is *material* for fiction and not the unadorned art object itself.

The three novels immediately following *Pillow of Grass—Sanshirō* (1908), *And Then* (*Sorekara,* 1909), and *The Gate* (*Mon,* 1910)—are usually called a trilogy, though not for any discernible reason, and are all third-person novels, less venturesome in technique than the earlier works. *Sanshirō,* the most explicitly social of the three, deals with the choice faced by an academically disillusioned student of English literature. There are three possibilities for his future endeavors: the world of Japan's past that existed until the early 1880s—tranquil but unexciting to him; the Western humanistic tradition; and third, the world of commerce, characterized by an enormous sexual vitality —obviously attractive, but very frightening. The novel traces Sanshirō's gradual awareness of his inability to choose a career and his bowing to the authority of a wise but unsuccessful teacher nicknamed "Great Darkness." The gloom that hangs over *Sanshirō* becomes heavier in the later novels, most noticeably in *The Gate,* whose quiet hero grumbles at the end, in response to his wife's pleasant notice of the coming of spring: "Yes, but it will soon be winter again." [9]

Sōseki is more experimental in his next three novels, *Until the Equinox* (*Higansugi made,* 1912), *The Wanderer* (*Kōjin,* 1913), and *The Heart* (*Kokoro,* 1914), which show him in his brilliant maturity. *Until the Equinox* is a series of episodes starting with a third-person narrative describing the detective work of a young student. It then moves on to the student's friend Sunaga and his family, whom the student spied on earlier. This is followed by Sunaga's first-person account of his relationship with his mother and his cousin. The series ends with another first-person story, this by Sunaga's uncle, which however contains letters from the nephew. Despite the shift in the narrative voice from one episode to the next, continuity is maintained by the use of a single listener, the student of the first story. Thus, in the course of the building tension among the voices, the central theme of love and loneliness in Sunaga's life becomes an aspect of the first student's mind as he takes it all in. The success of this novel comes largely from the haunting ambiguity of the multiple narrators amounting at times to a suggestive and elusive feeling of the double.

But Sōseki's multiple narrative arrangement is perhaps best utilized in *The Heart,* one of his finest novels. Here the "I," a student, tells the story of his friendship with the *sensei.** From the beginning there is the suggestion of the double, one the actualized and the other the potential of the same man—a motif often visible in Sōseki's works, as in many modern novels. The relationship has aspects of both the homosexual and the parental-filial, although at the same time the student is very curious about the older man, again like a detective.[10] He sees in the teacher what he wants to become; the teacher sees in the youth what he once was. The protagonist's search for a father, however, fails in various ways. First, his actual father becomes ill, and he has to leave the *sensei.* While he is in the country taking care of his father, he hears the news of the Emperor's death, in the context of the novel the Emperor Meiji being the universal father figure. There follows the loss of another father, General Nogi, hero of the Russo-Japanese War, who took his life to be with the Emperor in death. With all these father-figures leaving him all at once, the student is pushed to finish his growing up and get settled in life, and he writes asking his *sensei* for help in finding a job. The answer is a suicide note (albeit a rather lengthy one). He catches the first train back to Tokyo, leaving his father on his deathbed. The last part of the novel consists of the long letter of the sensei—an

---

* *Sensei* means literally "earlier born"; hence, master, teacher, guru. The term is applied to almost anybody nowadays. A *sensei* is not only a professor or spiritual guide, but anyone higher in seniority in almost any occupation. Thus politicians, writers, attorneys, and even entertainers are often called *sensei* by their younger associates.

autobiography really, telling of his loneliness, guilt, and love for his wife. He writes how he has always blamed himself for the suicide of his friend "K" (the initial of *Kokoro,* "The Heart"), who was in love with the girl who is now his wife. As K was then, the *sensei,* too, is now utterly lonely, and death is the only possible choice.

The book is remarkable for Sōseki's careful authorial withdrawal. Although the *sensei* is obviously a sympathetic character, there are moments where his egotism comes under the author's censure. So with the student. Both speak from a limited point of view, which only intensifies our need to apprehend a truth closer to the center of the novel but not disclosed.

What is most fascinating about the book, however, is Sōseki's near despair about the limits of communication, a feeling explicitly stated by the *sensei* at several points (for instance, Part III, chap. 39). And yet *The Heart* achieves its final effect in the language of silence. One memorable passage occurs (Part One, chap. 26) when the young man, having just finished his graduation thesis, takes the older man out for a walk on a beautiful spring afternoon. The two are of course fond of each other, but they are not really close; there is an invisible wall somehow separating them.

> There were also peonies covering an area of about ten *tsubo.* It was too early in the summer for them to be in bloom. At the edge of this field of peonies was an old bench. Sensei stretched himself out on it. I sat down on the end and began to smoke. Sensei gazed at the sky, which was so blue that it seemed transparent. I was fascinated by the young leaves that surrounded me. When I looked at them carefully, I found that no two trees had leaves of exactly the same color. The leaves of each maple tree, for instance, had their own distinctive coloring. Sensei's hat, which he had hung on top of a slender cedar sapling, was blown off by the breeze.[11]

The clear imagery of the scene surely contains "meaning," but without naming it. Its beauty is verbal, of course; symbolic, too. But all these named objects—transparent sky, young maple leaves, the fallen hat—bespeak their meaning as though requiring no words to mediate. It is not painterly, it is hardly literary. As in life itself, things address themselves directly to the reader. The force of the passage comes from its uttermost condensation of language to the thingness of the named, from the powerfully resonating *haiku* brevity and plainness.

Sōseki's steadily darkening vision of life is expressed in *Grass on the Wayside* (*Michikusa*, 1915), his last complete novel and his only I-novel in the sense that all the narrative events come from the actual history of his own life. This is not to say, however, that it banishes fiction entirely. In narrative selection as well as in the narrator's careful maintenance of distance from the characters, the work is imaginative in the most fundamental sense. Many Japanese claim it as their favorite of all Sōseki's works, and it also has supporters among American readers.[12] To me, however, it is the only tedious work he wrote. The main character, the author's surrogate, is an unpleasant egotist, petulant yet depressed, and overly preoccupied with money. Although the narrator makes clear that he is just as critical of the hero as the reader is, this does not relieve the dismal impression he creates. If a certain sincerity strikes the reader occasionally, it derives from the pitiful situation being presented, and not from the full persuasion of the Sōseki art. For me, *Grass on the Wayside* is interesting mostly because it differs so vastly from *Light and Darkness*, Sōseki's final effort, but also because this very difference suggests the discoveries he must have made during its writing, preparing him for the next undertaking.

Light and Darkness (*Meian*), like most of Sōseki's works, was serialized daily in the *Asahi* newspaper—in 188 sections from May 26, 1916, to December 14 of the same year, five days after his death. Daily serialization obviously differs from the monthly or even weekly installment form of the Dickensian novel, not to mention its differences from the publication of a whole work in book form. While a typical weekly installment—of, for instance, *Hard Times* or *Great Expectations*—runs to about a dozen modern-edition pages, each daily unit is of necessity extremely short, amounting in English translation to less than two pages.

With each unit, however abbreviated, requiring some autonomy, the whole work takes on the aspect of a mosaic pattern, the work comprising many uniform-sized tiny sections. Thus, there is a tendency toward sparseness in descriptive detail, even though one episode may range over several installments. Short installments affect the suspense element, too, which often appears like the couplet at the end of a sonnet. This is necessarily different from Dickens' use of suspense in his longer installments. Sōseki's work, in fact, with its regular occurrence of subtle surprise elements between units, gives an impression much like that of a grand sonnet sequence.

This is not to say, however, that, given its sonnet-sequence structure, *Light and Darkness* should be identified with the indigenous *haiku* or *waka* sequence (*renku* or *renga*). For this work, of all the Sōseki novels, perhaps of all the modern Japanese novels, comes closest to the orthodox Western novel.

Light and Darkness, the longest of Sōseki's novels even though incomplete, tells a story of only a few weeks' duration. The thirty-year-old hero, a corporation employee, finds he must have an operation for a fistula. There is a money problem arising from this unexpected medical expense, but this is only a symptom of the general budgetary pattern in his household, relating to his wife's taste for luxury and his vanity that encourages it. After the operation, the hero goes to a hot spring to recuperate, where he arranges to meet the woman he was in love with before his marriage. Soon after their encounter, the book breaks off, leaving scarcely a clue as to subsequent development.[13] The story being so uneventful, the drama of the novel is intensely psychological. And what makes it unique in modern Japanese literature is that its characters have discernible personalities, which most novelistic characters, especially those of the I-novel, very rarely achieve.

The notion of personality is quite different to a Japanese from what it is to a Westerner. Whether he will become an electronics worker, a teacher of English in a high school, or a fish-processing worker on a whaler, the young Japanese studies his assigned role till he perfects it. His worth will be measured by his approximation to the ideal of his type (*the* teacher, *the* electronics worker, *the* fisherman)—"Sensei wa sensei rashiku shiro" (Be like the teacher you are). Personality is thus not a valued seed to be nurtured into flower, but a bud that must be "withered" (*kareta*) as soon as it shows itself. At maturity, having been tamed in this way from early childhood, the Japanese "personality," like an age-old redwood *bonsai*, ought to be a truly balanced and pleasing form.

Since the Meiji era, with Western philosophies of individualism and egalitarianism being increasingly propagated in Japanese society, strict role-definition has loosened to an extent. Probably the greatest difference takes the form of today's much increased inter-generational mobility (a tenant farmer's second son becoming a cabinet minister), which does not touch the reorganization of the vertical structure itself. As Nakane Chie so persuasively argues in *Japanese Society,* the old vertical organization has survived almost intact in today's highly corporate and industrialized Japan.

Such a society still fosters a high degree of ritualism in everyday activities, whether economic, social, or cultural, as can be seen in the disciplined style and movement of the *noh* play as well as in the high development of the honorific system in the Japanese language. It also encourages the deep and wide establishment of whatever common myth is circulating, as recent Japanese history shows very clearly: the disastrous national dream of military glory has been followed by the concerted passion for industrial preeminence. If such national programs do not invariably capture the imagination of writers and intellectuals, this does not mean the latter have any real alternatives to offer. Even the traditional religions manage to do little more than affirm collective enterprise and discourage individualism.

Japanese society does not, in short, promote the necessary condition for growth of the novelistic imagination: the egalitarian sensibility that sees a unique human personality in powerful statesman and day-laborer alike. Instead, people are regarded according to their assigned social slots. One is a noodle-truck driver or a university professor before one is Yamada Tarō or Kimura Hanako, and is, accordingly, comical or dignified, disreputable or respectable, on a subtly shaded scale of social connotation. The novel, on the other hand, in order to explore the inverted universe that an individual consciousness is, always pulls toward freeing people from their role characteristics, and it is against such energy that Japanese society works so relentlessly with its tribalism and ceremonialism.

Novelists need people—men and women with their own motivations, their own mannerisms, their own style of intelligence, their own unique expression and appearance. The problem for the Japanese novelist is that there is no general acknowledgement in his culture that noticeable personalities should be allowed to exist. A carpenter who sounds like Adam Bede or a governess who behaves like Jane Eyre—not to say a gamekeeper who acts out like Oliver Mellors—will not only be disapproved of morally but disbelieved artistically as well. (The situation is not unlike that prevailing at an early stage in the development of the European novel.) From this impasse, the writer frequently falls back on his own kind for his character types, déclassé writers and intellectuals, who offer several advantages. First, they are a new category of people, unknown before the Meiji importations from the West, and thus there is greater freedom in defining them in the social hierarchy. Second, and in part because they are a new class, writers and intellectuals really are freer in attitude and behavior than conventional middle-class people. Third, using the life style and character types of his own kind allows the writer to deal with what he supposedly knows best.

But even this more liberated and liberally regarded class presents some problems upon adoption into the world of fiction. One concerns their usual sense of alienation from the society at large; the other, the interior of the writer's "personality."

We recall that "Futabatei Shimei" meant "drop dead" in no uncertain terms. But the writer has been a social outcast, "dead" to the world, from the beginning of modern literature in Japan. No doubt, even in Victorian society (which bears better comparison in many ways with modern Japan than present-day America or England does) writers felt a degree of disenchantment. And yet a Mill or an Arnold still felt himself an active member of the society he chastised. He was still an established insider. Contrastingly, the alienated Japanese writers, having dropped out more completely and visibly, were given up on by the society and were thus more bitterly isolated. Rare is the man like Mori Ogai or even Sōseki, who kept a successful career going within the establishment all the while he was writing. More usual are the writers who associated themselves almost exclusively with other writers and artists, and who suffered from— or enjoyed—the three common conditions of an artist's fate— poverty, loneliness, and a certain degree of sexual freedom. Not bothering to acquaint themselves with most people's ordinary activities of life, they lived lives which were narrow in perspective and extremely limited in variety. And when they wrote their counterparts into their fiction as rebels and outcasts, they tended to repeat these same patterns monotonously.

The notion of the inner self, whether that of author or his character, throws a more serious impediment in the way of the novel's development in Japan. Japanese writers are essentially lonely souls who in their inward search for the core of existence often identify themselves with a Dostoevsky or a Rilke. And yet, in finally facing themselves, they discover a strange emptiness. Long accustomed to viewing the self as a blemish on Nature, their Buddhist tradition inclines them not to define and assert the borders of the self, but to long for the obliteration of such outlines in a fusion with the All. And Nature, through ceremony, can offer a substitute in which the ancient collective experience of the people can be relived. Ironically, such ceremony is the genius of modern Japan. There is another irony, and a bitter one, that the alienated writers should be found to be even more loyal to this ceremony, little else by now but the ghost of the collective memory, than the establishment men and women who would promote the myth.

Writers often refuse to see such irony, however, by obfuscating the fact that their "self" is much more the heritage of Confucius and Buddha than the modern self of Descartes and Nietzsche. Similarly, they often mistakenly identify the seductive Buddhist nothingness with a post-Christian stoicism. Unfortunately, such misidentifications have had fairly serious personal consequences. The imported view of the self distorts the meaning of moral action as of art—as we will see in the discussion of Dazai Osamu

and Mishima Yukio. It is a high price these writers have paid
for an imported product, and to some extent the value received
has not been commensurate with the cost. The modern Japanese
novel, not yet succeeding in penetrating the inner life of its
national identity, has likewise been unable to develop consistently
authentic novelistic characters with an identifiable personal core.

Up until his very last work, characterization in Sōseki's novels
follows pretty much the same pattern as that of his fellow novelists. In *Pillow of Grass* both the poet-painter and the elusive
heroine are presented as facets of a single attitude rather than
as full and distinct personalities. Even in *The Heart,* the young
man and the *sensei* are more functions of the mind than two real
people, and as such they are conducive, as in a romance, to rich
symbolic interpretations, but not to dramatic development. In
Light and Darkness, however, Sōseki for the first time creates a
world in which novelistic characters breathe and feel and talk
just like people one might know. Where does their authenticity
come from?

In *Grass on the Wayside* Sōseki began to experiment with full
characterization. Kenzō, the author's surrogate, is scrutinized in
detail psychologically as well as morally, as is his wife, the author's wife's surrogate, who is one of the very few complete
characterizations, female or male, in the whole Sōseki canon. It
is as though for the sake of the analytical novel that the author
proceeds systematically to dissect himself. Here he seems especially to be perfecting his skill in voice modulation, all the while
keeping himself clearly apart from the characters. In *Light and
Darkness* he goes further, abandoning the stance of the omniscient narrator and adopting instead the dramatic mode of individuals speaking with their own voices.* Each character thinks
and feels, and wonders about the others, and the narrator conveys
with remarkable sensitivity each one's uncertainties about himself and others. The characters are islands of self-consciousness
in the novel, rising up from the deep that separates them, and
connects them.

* The novel has been translated by V. H. Viglielmo (see note 14).

The book opens on the scene of the doctor palpating Tsuda's fistula. We are not told what Tsuda's physical sensations are during this examination; only his response to the doctor's prognosis is given. Going home, Tsuda recalls what the pain is like, but the people on the streetcar do not even know he exists. The opening thus establishes the basic scheme of existence in *Light and Darkness*: a man's most private sensation (which he often conceals even from himself), posed against his awareness of others, posed in turn against his recognition of others' unawareness of himself. Superimposed on this is a question which will be raised repeatedly: "Why did she [Tsuda's former sweetheart] marry him [another man]? She must have wanted to. But she wasn't supposed to. And why did I marry her [Onobu, his own wife]? The marriage must have come about because I wanted it. But I hadn't wanted to marry her." (Chap. 4.)[14] We can never know what another person is to himself, and when we fully understand that fact, our certainty about our own self-understanding, too, is threatened.

Tsuda and Onobu's marriage, the central relationship of the novel, is very intricately understood by Sōseki, as the next incident, apparently of small significance, shows. Tsuda arrives home from the medical examination to see his wife in front of their house in expectation of his return. The minute she sees him, however, she turns away from him slightly, facing straight ahead and appearing to be looking at something. It seems to him she feigns surprise when he asks her what she is looking at: "Oh, you frightened me," she says, "Welcome home." (My translation.) She then tells him she was watching some sparrows, and Tsuda can see no evidence of these. Tsuda possibly interprets her behavior as a form of "coquetry" not unusual in a new bride, although this possibility is only vaguely suggested by the mention of "his wife's coquetry" as applied to the whole situation. Onobu's response in turn is not given either, except that she proceeds at once to the next items on her agenda of wifely ministrations: relieving her husband of his walking stick, opening the door for him, helping him change clothes. Maybe she takes it for granted that her flirtatiousness is natural in the situation and that he will take it at that. But we cannot be sure.

Light and Darkness is almost clinically precise in measuring degrees of taciturnity corresponding to the uncertainties in human relationships. The reader is never given an easy summary of complex interactions between people. The interaction of Tsuda and Onobu, for instance, could be analyzed as: Tsuda's sensation/ feeling/ understanding; Tsuda's feeling for Onobu; Tsuda's understanding of Onobu and his attitude toward it; Tsuda's understanding of her understanding of him and her attitude toward it, as well as his feeling for it; Tsuda's understanding of Onobu's understanding of his understanding of her and his attitude toward it, and his attitude toward this whole understanding. Then, the whole process must be repeated on Onobu's side: Onobu's sensation/ feeling/ understanding; Onobu's feeling for Tsuda, and so on. We are given clues to these levels and gradations of self-consciousness at every stage of the novel, the first 44 chapters being from Tsuda's perspective, the next 47 from Onobu's, and the remainder alternating between the two. Tsuda thus conjectures about Onobu, as Onobu conjectures about him, and yet the narrator never lapses into any facile guarantee about the rightness or wrongness of either one's conjecture about the other. He seldom even compares the two versions, since that would imply his omniscience. Thus the irony does not principally operate on the discrepancies between the two sets of conjectures, but elsewhere. It is almost as if to say that the more intelligent and self-conscious one is, the more completely one is cut off from others; the more luminous one's self-awareness, the darker the world around. We are of course not told this explicitly, but the novel effects this dark separation through a specific narrative technique, that of indirection and silence.

Of the major characters, Tsuda is the most unpleasant. He is a role-player, being many different things to different people. With a habitat well below the level of interpersonal relating, he prefers always to understand his understanding of Onobu's understanding of his understanding of her, and so on. The heavy-knotted fabric of his self-consciousness incapacitates him for the experience of any direct emotion. Nonetheless, he thinks he can read other people. When he discloses to his wife, for instance, his plan to go to a resort without her, he believes he is able to manipulate her by controlling the amount and type of information she gets. Meanwhile, he is totally unable to feel her craving for his love and her loneliness for lack of it. She is mostly for him an object of observation, not someone to feel with or feel for. Ironically, it is his own performance, not hers, that becomes increasingly transparent to more and more people as the novel progresses. The overbearing Mrs. Yoshikawa sees through his mask (chap. 141), as does his humorless sister (chap. 102) and his sardonic friend Kobayashi (chap. 166). And with each successive uncovering of his motives, Tsuda appears progressively more vulnerable.

Although Tsuda is not explicitly interpreted for us, his gradual physical recovery suggests the possibility of a parallel spiritual recovery. It is notable, for instance, that his meeting with Kiyoko, the girl he was in love with before his marriage to Onobu, is preceded by an unexpected self-encounter. Returning from the bath, he loses his way in the maze of hallways, and he is suddenly confronted by a "ghost":

> He soon turned away from the water. Then, since with the same glance he suddenly encountered a man's form, he gave a start, and stared at it. But it was only the image of himself reflected in the large mirror hung by the side of the wash basins. The mirror was almost as tall as an average man. And, like one in a barber's shop, it was hung upright. Consequently, not only the reflection of his face but that of his shoulders, waist, and hips as well, were on the same plane as he was, and faced him directly. Even after he realized that it was himself he was looking at, he still did not remove his eyes from the mirror. He noticed that he was rather pale, even though he had just come from the bath, but he was at a loss to know why. Since he had neglected to have a haircut for some time, his hair was bushy and unkempt. It shone like lacquer because it was freshly wet from the bath, and for some reason he thought it looked like a garden after it has been devastated by a windstorm. (P. 345)

Having been so "lost," Tsuda does not really know the "meaning" of this experience, nor do we for sure. But he does seem to be perceiving just a small crack on the smooth surface of his mask as he begins to "retrace his steps." Precisely at this moment he sees Kiyoko at the top of the staircase, like Beatrice in the *Vita Nuova*. There is the suggestion, then, that he might begin to accept the isolating darkness and thus be himself more fully. Only the merest suggestion, though, just as in life we are never allowed any clearer foresight than the ghost of a hint.

This careful matching of narrative concealment and disclosure to people's knowledge of one another in actual life is certainly the most important feature in the characterization of *Light and Darkness*. It is a precision which gives life to its characters and a mystery of being to their existence that extends well beyond the pages of the novel spatially and temporally. Judgment is urged but not imposed on us, while all the provided bases for judgment contain the uncertainty always present in the act of human judgment.

As for Onobu, she is one of the most attractive women in the Japanese novel, being unusually intelligent for a female character in that tradition. Although her explanation to herself of her sole motivation—to win her husband's love—is subjected to some further scrutiny, it is evident that she is genuinely concerned with him. She is shrewd and calculating to a degree, and she too performs, but she is aware of these traits in herself and is vulnerable because of that knowledge. And then she knows her vulnerability also, which is probably what makes her so much more attractive a personality than her husband.

There is a scene in which her usually well-guarded defenses nearly break down, and she pleads with Tsuda to give her complete confidence in him:

> She suddenly cried out:
> "I *want* to trust you. I *want* to put my mind at ease. I want to trust you more than you can imagine."
> "Are you saying I can't imagine?"
> "No, you can't possibly. Because if you could, you'd have to change. Since you can't imagine, you're as unconcerned as you are."

"I'm not unconcerned!"

"Well, you certainly aren't sorry for me and you don't have any pity on me."

"What do you mean by feeling sorry for you or having pity on you?"

After he had in effect rejected her criticism, he was quiet for a while. He then faltered a bit as he attempted to evade the issue.

"You say I'm not concerned about you—no matter how much I actually am. Because you can be sure that if there's reason to be I will be. But if there isn't, what am I supposed to do?"

Her voice trembled with tension.

"Oh, Yoshio, listen to me!"

He said nothing.

"Please tell me I don't have to worry, I beg of you. Put my mind at ease and rescue me, because I have no one else to turn to but you. I'm helpless, and I'll die if you turn me aside. So please say I can put my mind at ease. Just one word will do, but please say I don't have to worry."

"Everything's all right. Don't worry, I tell you." (Pp. 286–87)

Significantly, the energy and intelligence of this passage derives less from Onobu's character—vital as that is—than from our knowledge of her uncertainty about her husband. We see her craving his total reassurance, and when he rations out something very partial—"Everything's all right. Don't worry . . ."—she cannot be satisfied and fights for more. Tsuda, of course, who doesn't know how much she knows about his past and how much she doesn't, somehow manages to protect his façade by shortweighting her demand for reassurance every time. Sōseki knows precisely the quality and amount of each one's ignorance of the other. And although he puts us close to that privileged position, he leaves ample space for uncertainties and ambiguities.

Ohide, Tsuda's self-centered sister, is a forceful but also subtle person, able to ferret out the childish elements in her brother's and his wife's behavior. She bullies them singlehandedly, all the while unaware of her own deep commitment to the confrontation.

The hospital scene (chaps. 104–110) where Tsuda and Onobu defend their financial judgment against Ohide's criticism is interesting in several ways. First, Tsuda's antiseptic recovery-room, charged with intense emotion (there are two more visitors later on, Kobayashi and Mrs. Yoshikawa), is a perfect reflection of the hero's personality, which passively registers and reacts to things rather than actively taking the initiative. Second, the scene sensitively presents the separate thoughts and feelings of three very different people. Third, at any given moment, we are able to see the one person alert to the other two while not quite knowing, however, exactly what their thoughts and feelings are about himself.

The individual as basically alone—this, as I have mentioned earlier, is the general outlook of *Light and Darkness* on human relationship. Chapter 106, for instance, turns the narrative into a drama script in which there is hardly any narrative comment on the inner responses of the three main characters. As in a drama, their relationship is formed and defined in the intervals between the speeches and the space behind the speeches rather than in narrated passages providing such information and an attitude on it. The result is—somewhat more subtly here than in the typical example of this terseness, a Hemingway novel—both an increased objectivity and an intensified sense of their isolation one from another. Even more significant is the reader's realization of *his* distance from the characters, owing directly to this increased need to conjecture their every reaction.

My meaning will perhaps be clearer if the scene in the recovery room is compared with one from a novel in a different tradition:

> Maggie gave the tips of her fingers, and said, "Quite well, thank you," in a tone of proud indifference. Philip's eyes were watching them keenly; but Lucy was used to seeing variations in their manner to each other, and only thought with regret that there was some natural antipathy which every now and then surmounted their mutual good-will. "Maggie is not the sort of woman Stephen admires, and she is irritated by something in him which she inter-

prets as conceit," was the silent observation that accounted for everything to guileless Lucy. Stephen and
Maggie had no sooner completed this studied greeting
than each felt hurt by the other's coldness. And Stephen,
while rattling on in questions to Philip about his recent
sketching expedition, was thinking all the more about
Maggie because he was not drawing her into the conversation as he had invariably done before. "Maggie and
Philip are not looking happy," thought Lucy: "this first
interview has been saddening to them." (George Eliot,
The Mill on the Floss)[15]

Here we have a scene involving several people all desperately trying to guess each other's thoughts. But in this work there is a
strong voice letting us know that she at least knows her characters' minds. The omniscient narrator can in this way serve as a
sort of communal voice linking the separate members into a single
understanding which is then confidently offered the reader, who is
in turn reassured. Like belief in the omniscience of God, there is
operating in this tradition an implicit faith in the author's presentation which is assumed by both reader and author. What separates Henry James from George Eliot is the withering away of
this assumption that the narrator is voicing shared concerns and
interests dealing with everybody's business. And Sōseki, in this
novel at least, takes his place on our side of the breakdown.

It is for this reason that the similarities often found between
Sōseki and Jane Austen are not quite accurate.[16] There is no doubt
that he experimented with what she had done novelistically a
century earlier: her stern moral stand relentlessly exploding her
characters' self-illusion, her abstract diction, her nonphysical, non-
visual description, precise syntax, and deceptively simple dialogue
—all these techniques are used in *Light and Darkness*. Even that
subversive irony directed at the unwary reader as well as the characters is also in evidence. And yet the important distinction between *Light and Darkness* and *Emma* or *Pride and Prejudice* is
its loss, through rejection of narrative authority, of the community
of the novel which draws the characters into a world shared with
each other and with the reader.

There are two other characters—Mrs. Yoshikawa, the wife of

Tsuda's employer, and Tsuda's friend Kobayashi—who deserve some comment. Mrs. Yoshikawa is a thoroughly alive, enjoyable person, confident, overbearing, and shrewd. She overwhelms the passive Tsuda, and punctures his self-illusion, I believe to our pleasure. Up to the point where she visits Tsuda in the hospital, her quasi-maternal domination, her busybody curiosity and cavils are all put into a perfectly understandable context. But her scenario-writing for Tsuda's reunion with his old love is quite something else. Her motives for this are much too unclear: can she be that much interested in Tsuda's simply clarifying the circumstances of the end of his affair? Or is she simply trying to help him recover his spiritual buoyancy? Maybe. But at the risk of his losing Onobu? Does she hate Onobu that much? And if so, why? Sōseki does not let us in on her secrets.

We do notice, however, that as Mrs. Yoshikawa plots the reunion, she becomes the plot-maker of the novel itself. Tsuda, at her suggestion (order?), is lifted out of the Onobu-Ohide-himself stalemate to face a new situation in a new setting. Mrs. Yoshikawa in a sense rescues the book at this point by bullying Tsuda into a new experience. As a character, she is no longer a likable self-indulgent woman, but a rich and powerful and exploitative one. And by this change she becomes a novelistic device, a dea ex machina who in coercing Tsuda coerces the novel.

Mrs. Yoshikawa's transformation has some bearing on another character of a type new in Sōseki's novels. A down-at-the-heel, rather unattractive journalist, Kobayashi appears to have emigrated right out of Dostoevsky's underground. Sōseki's fiction has almost always dealt with middle-class life style, which is generally a comfortable one, if occasionally hard up for money. Kobayashi's background is different: though he is well enough educated to be a professional, his origins are lower class. He also happens to be a rude, jealous, angry, brazen, irritable, cynical, and, with all this, admittedly lonely fellow. He has no steady job, feels his disorganized poverty acutely, and is so dependent on his friends that even his scheme of going to Korea to look for work depends on his getting their help. In return, he despises them. He attacks Tsuda's snobbery every way he knows how and almost resorts to blackmailing him to get what he wants.

Etō Jun is no doubt right in seeing the social victim in Kobayashi, the outcast writer type who attracted Sōseki's interest and
sympathy more and more toward the end of his life. According to
Etō, the author of *Light and Darkness* is in transition from being
a writer concerned with the self in the universe to one interested
in the self in society. Etō's thesis is right insofar as he disputes
several critics and biographers, such as Komiya Hōryū, Karaki
Junzō, and Takizawa Katsumi, who interpret the later Sōseki in
the light of his favorite dictum, *sokuten kyoshi* (accord to the
heavens, depart from the self), as if the slogan described what was
in fact the case with him and his work.[17] It does not. Sōseki is
neither saintly nor selfless, and to identify an author's aspirations
with the reality of the man is clearly absurd. At the same time,
Etō's interpretation of Kobayashi as the champion of Sōseki's
newly awakened social conscience is a bit overdrawn. The down-
and-out journalist's alienation and loneliness never develop significantly beyond that into full political consciousness. Etō talks
about Kobayashi's feeling for working-class people, citing the bar-
room scene (chap. 34). But I wonder if Kobayashi genuinely has
love for the workers or is merely using his firsthand acquaintance
with their life style to intimidate a middle-class snob like Tsuda.
Isn't Etō's great socialist hero in fact rather condescending to the
"lower orders," the same working-class people for whom he claims
to "have a great deal of sympathy" and whom he likes to meet in
such "wonderfully plebeian" places? Kobayashi the victim invites
the author's—and the reader's—sympathy for his misfortunes,
but he cannot carry the burden of Sōseki's mature social or political philosophy. Maybe he is fundamentally one of those shadowy characters who, operating on the symbolic level, haunt the
heroes of novels everywhere, like their darker self-images, their
doubles.

Earlier I mentioned Mrs. Yoshikawa's manipulation of Tsuda
and its effect on the plot. I think it notable that in their relationship Tsuda is the victim, whereas between him and Kobayashi we
find Tsuda is the exploiter, who can afford to be aloof, contemptuous, manipulative. Of course, he does not succeed in brandishing
his power nearly so well as Mrs. Yoshikawa does. (Actually, Kobayashi's uncanny insight sometimes almost frightens Tsuda, but

theirs is one of those relationships of master and servant, as Hegel saw it, where the servant is able at several points to overturn the master psychologically.) Nonetheless, the chain of exploitation runs through the whole society of this novel. And with Mrs. Yoshikawa as the bully of the whole book we cannot help but feel that Sōseki's dark irony is directed on the capitalism of Taishō Japan, which, as we are seeing, encroaches on the development of the novel itself.

Sōseki's near despair for human relationship permeates this last, unfinished novel, and yet we sense also the compassion of the man who can see, if darkly, the painfully clear boundaries of the modern self. It is in this sense that the Japanese novel has developed a mind not in the least impenetrable to the West—an unusual achievement, since most other novelists have worked within the familiar native consciousness. It is important that we not attribute Sōseki's performance solely to his knowledge of English literature; clearly at its root is his extraordinary personality, his very mind and heart. But in the light of those lifelong painful doubts of his about his claim to English, it may not be such an irrelevant tribute to suggest that Sōseki had indeed learned well the literature of England.

Part Two

Words dry and riderless,
The indefatigable hoof-taps.
While
From the bottom of the pool, fixed stars
Govern a life.
                    —SYLVIA PLATH, "Words"

Making no sound
   Yet smouldering with passion
      The firefly is still sadder
         Than the moaning insect.
            —MINAMOTO SHIGEYUKI

            It was her voice that made
The sky acutest at its vanishing.
She measured to the hour its solitude.
She was the single artificer of the world
In which she sang. And when she sang, the sea,
Whatever self it had, became the self
That was her song, for she was the maker.
               —WALLACE STEVENS,
                  "The Idea of Order at Key West"

Did it yell
      till it became all voice?
         Cicada-shell.
               —BASHŌ

IV

THE MARGINS OF LIFE

KAWABATA YASUNARI: *Snow Country*
and *The Sound of the Mountain*
—*I am a citizen of a lost country.*

Mr. Kawabata, as everyone knows, is a great stylist, but I believe he is finally a novelist without a style. Because style for the novelist means the will to interpret the world and discover the key to it. To arrange the world, separate it, and bring it out of chaos and angst into the narrow framework of form, the novelist has no other tool than style. . . . What is . . . a work of art, like Kawabata's masterpiece, which is a perfection in itself, but has abandoned the will to interpret the world so entirely? It fears no chaos, no angst. But its fearlessness is like the fearlessness of a silk string suspended before the void. It is the extreme opposite of the plastic will of the Greek sculptors who committed themselves to the permanence of marble; it is in sharp contrast to the fear that the harmonic Greek sculpture fights with its whole body.

Thus Mishima Yukio on Kawabata Yasunari, in 1958.[1] Like so much of Mishima's work, the comment shows a remarkable critical acuity. Yet I am bound finally to disagree. While it is true that Kawabata's poise is unshakable and that, unlike most Japanese novelists of the last fifty years, he does not feel compelled to scream his *Weltanschauung* at us, nor sermonize, nor organize, it does not follow that he has no "will to interpret the world." My crucial difference with Mishima, then, lies in how we see this "style," which is at once powerfully idiosyncratic and subtly suffused with a rich sense of life.

Early in his career Kawabata Yasunari (1899–1972) was a member of the Neo-Perceptionist school (Shin Kankaku Ha). The existence of this group, as a part of Japanese literary history, is not so interesting or important in itself: its creed, like those of the Naturalists, the Anti-Naturalists, and other groups, derives from imported avant-garde European manifestoes, and, like most, suffers from poor digestion of same. Thrown into their modernist mélanges are bits and dollops of Paul Morand, Andreyev, Croce, Bergson, futurism, cubism, expressionism, dadaism, symbolism, structuralism, realism, Strindberg, Swinburne, Hauptmann, Romain Rolland, Schnitzler, Lord Dunsany, Wilde, Lady Gregory, and a lot else*—all assembled, presumably, to spice the domestic literary staples, but in fact to preserve a conservative aesthetic against the encroaching Marxists. Most of its members are now forgotten (with the exception of Yokomitsu Riichi, who, however, became a very different sort of writer later on), and Kawabata's position in the group was not a dominant one. Nonetheless, when looked at as a serious attempt at enlarging the novelistic possibilities of the Japanese language, the modernist practices of the group must be recognized as vital in the formation of Kawabata's style.

Kawabata's main contribution to the group's platform, "The New Tendency of the Avant-Garde Writers" (*Shinshin Sakka no Shinkeikō Kaisetsu*), published in 1925, makes a plea for the new

* Conspicuously absent from this list are names such as Cocteau, Breton, Eliot, Joyce, Gide, Valéry, Rilke, all of whom were introduced and translated within the next few years. The list is garnered from references in the collection of articles by members of the group such as Chiba Kameo, Kataoka Teppei, Kawabata Yasunari, Akaki Kensuke, Inagaki Sokuho, Yokomitsu Riichi, and Nii Kaku in vol. 67 of the Nippon Gendai Bungaku Zenshū series, *Shin Kankaku Ha Bungaku Shū* (Tokyo: Kōdansha, 1968), which is also my text for the discussion of Neo-Perceptionism.

—new perception, new expression, and new style—and strongly emphasizes the importance of sense perception for the novelist. While not being very precise in his "epistemology of expressionism," and dodging most of the hard problems of his theme, Kawabata does spell out the need for a new language to replace the existing "lifeless, objective narrative language." "Dadaist," "Freudian," "free associative," "subjective, intuitive, and sensuous" expression—all such terms are left undefined, but in the context of his discussion they do suggest a coherent feeling for a certain style. He would have a language for the novel that would reflect immediately the inchoate state of a man's thoughts, feelings, and sensory experience. Instead of syntactically complete sentences, the characters (or the narrator) ought to be allowed to speak sometimes in fragments, which will not only suggest more accurately the author's view of the particular situation but will give the reader a fuller picture of the characters and their surroundings. In such a language, the seer is not yet separated from the seen, the speaker from the spoken. To illustrate his point, Kawabata provides a sample sentence or two ("My eyes were red roses" as preferable to "My eyes saw red roses"), but unfortunately this tends to muddle the discussion more than clarify it.[2]

Another member of the school was a little more articulate on this same point. According to Kataoka Teppei, "The small stations along the line were ignored like pebbles" effectively expresses the train's speed, whereas an ordinary statement like "The express rushed along without stopping at any station," though referring to the same observation, is merely reportorial. In the latter sentence, there is no relationship "between the express train, the small stations, and the author's own feeling," whereas the Neo-Perceptionist version allows the author's immediate perception, and the reader's, to flow with the movement of the train. It also provides, Kataoka says, a way for the writer to recover his own individuality from the "general, commonsensical, and public" language ordinarily so resistant to the individual's imprint.

I am not sure that even this argument is really persuasive—perhaps because the example of "The small stations along the line . . ." is undistinguished, Neo-Perceptionist or not.* Besides, the singularity of a particular expression, its oddness, does not guarantee its liveliness or perceptual precision, or even its individuality. We are aware of course that these arguments flourished around 1920, about the time the imagists and vorticists and a variety of dadaists were urging basic changes in literary language. Thus, the apparent vagueness and confusion on the part of the Neo-Perceptionists are, without being unduly sympathetic, quite understandable. If their arguments seem to us now of rather modest significance, the efforts of these writers in behalf of a responsive novelistic language was nonetheless beneficial to its development.

What is really curious about the whole movement is that its exponents regarded the whole rationale of their movement as Western in origin, and felt that the recommended changes were only a further step in the inevitable westernization of the novel —a Western art—and the language of the novel. Besides Kawabata and Kataoka, other Neo-Perceptionists read and rehashed the arguments they found in European and American literary journals, while ignoring the lessons of their own tradition to be found in the *haiku* and *waka*—those arts of suggestion and evocation, reversal and juxtaposition, so deeply rooted in the alogical, intuitive, and "irrational" sensibility of the East itself. By expedition into their own tradition they might have realized a sufficient freeing of the "reportorial narrative" prose without moving all the way to a distortion of idiomatic Japanese. Or if they had read Ezra Pound—or indeed Ernest Fenollosa, who lived in Japan for fifteen years toward the end of the century—they would have learned that what the European surrealists were searching for existed in their very own indigenous poetic method consisting of the *haiku* and *waka* and the ideogrammic form. But the young Kawabata and his friends were much too bent on "modernizing"

---

* Aside from the eccentricity of the expression, the sentence is taken out of context. Kataoka's model sentence, in the original written by a young writer, is preceded by "It is high noon. The packed special express train was running at full speed." As Kataoka presents it, the sentence is supposed to contain all the information which is in fact given by the very ordinary antecedent sentence. Although this model has been frequently quoted by scholars, no one seems to have noticed the Neo-Perceptionist's error.

their art to notice what lay so close at hand.* In their view, the course of Japanese literature was to run more or less straight from the "conventional" narrative entertainment to naturalism, to proletarian literature, and to surrealism, just as the Japanese theorists had read was the course for the European literatures.³

The imprint of Neo-Perceptionism on Kawabata continues strong in those works written over the ten years following this "modernist" manifesto. Stories and longer works like "The Ghost of the Rose" (*Bara no Yūrei*, 1927), *The Red Gang of Asakusa* (*Asakusa Kurenai-Dan*, 1929–30), "Needle and Glass and Fog" (*Hari to Garasu to Kiri*, 1930), and "The Crystal Fantasy" (*Suishō Gensō*, 1931), to mention only a few, are all marked by boldly experimental features. The deformation of idioms, such as in the sentence "an illness entered the core of the body"⁴ in "Needle and Glass and Fog"; a long interior monologue, very much after Molly Bloom's, in "The Crystal Fantasy"; the predominantly nominal and asyntactic construction of *The Red Gang of Asakusa;* the hundred miniature "novels" later collected into one volume as *The Palm-Sized Stories* (*Tanagokoro no Shōsetsu*, 1922–50)—these are the most conspicuous examples. Determinedly "modern" too are their themes and settings. The characters are typically urban "new types," whose life style is self-consciously "Western." The wife in "The Crystal Fantasy," for example, living in a "Western" room with "Western" furniture, sits at her dressing table polishing her nails and looking out on her greenhouse. Her stream of consciousness could be that of a European woman, since, with the exception of one mention each of Tokyo, a Japanese writer, and a Japanese swimmer in the strange catalogue of items several pages long, the story is quite cosmopolitan in its references.

I do not mean, of course, that in these experiments Kawabata succeeds in creating anything like the cosmopolitan as a type of

---

* The relationship between imagism and Japanese literature (and Chinese ideograms) has been discussed by many critics. The best book on the subject remains Ernest Fenollosa's *The Chinese Written Character as a Medium for Poetry,* ed. Ezra Pound, collected in Pound's *Instigations* (New York: Boni and Liveright, 1920), pp. 357–88. See Pound's numerous comments on the ideogrammic method in his earlier books and Hugh Kenner's *The Poetry of Ezra Pound* (Norfolk, Conn.: New Directions, 1951).

person recognizable across all linguistic and cultural borders. The notion of a cosmopolitan is itself quite specific to modern Western culture. The fact is, in the complexion of their feelings and emotions his characters are unmistakably Japanese. "The Crystal Fantasy," for instance, puts the cosmopolitan wife in the context of a tension between her medical and scientific interests and her sexual fantasies—in itself an unlikely situation for a Japanese woman of the time—and yet her relationship to her husband at once defines her as Japanese. There is a very uncomfortable gap in the work between its intellectual intention and its actualization by a sensibility formed out of the traditional expectation and response. Whatever stylistic feat Neo-Perceptionism may have achieved here, one realizes, it is not so much surrealistic in effect as *haiku*-like, still imbued as it is with the age-old associations and conventions despite its being set in a modern frame of reference. Natsume Sōseki undoubtedly knew this a generation before, and Kawabata, too, came to know it as he matured. For all its youthful wrongheaded theorizing, Neo-Perceptionism taught Kawabata a great deal about the possibilities of Japanese for prose fiction, as we will see in our discussion of *Snow Country* and *The Sound of the Mountain*.

One of Kawabata's earliest and least experimental stories, "The Izu Dancer" (*Izu no Odoriko*, 1926), stands up better than his modernist attempts. Like *Pillow of Grass*, "The Izu Dancer" is a first-person story of a trip to the country. Unlike the Sōseki story, however, the voice here is lyrical throughout, and not mediated either by irony or by manipulation of time between the events and the telling. The student-narrator's experience is set in the fresh provincial scene by means of an evocative, slightly nostalgic language which is neither elaborate nor learned. While *Pillow of Grass* is a complex experiment in the narrative sequence, "The Izu Dancer" has the forthright appearance of a single unadorned episode. There is more quiet understatement and less surprise. And, finally, as against Sōseki's hero who moves from uninvolvement toward greater involvement, Kawabata's moves in the other direction, toward less involvement.

The student is attracted to a girl in a traveling family of dancer-entertainers whom he meets while on vacation, but he does not exactly know what he wants from the encounter. Right away, he realizes he is tormented with the thought of her "entertaining" her clients. Next morning, however, as a fierce storm clears, he sees her nude in the outdoor bath:

> One small figure ran out into the sunlight and stood for a moment at the edge of the platform calling something to us, arms raised as though for a plunge into the river. It was the little dancer. I looked at her, at the young legs, at the sculptured white body, and suddenly a draught of fresh water seemed to wash over my heart. I laughed happily. She was a child, a mere child, a child who could run out naked into the sun and stand there on her tiptoes in her delight at seeing a friend. I laughed on, a soft, happy laugh. It was as though a layer of dust had been cleared from my head. And I laughed on and on. It was because of her too-rich hair that she had seemed older, and because she was dressed like a girl of fifteen or sixteen. I had made an extraordinary mistake indeed.[5]

No longer threatened by the need to discover and test his sexuality, the "I" really comes to love the girl as they roam from one mountain village to another in the company of her family. She responds to his affection, and they discover very gentle and tender feelings for each other. The story ends as they part and the young man returns to school.

There are several episodes which are seemingly unrelated to the main line of the story. One is toward the end where another boy, bound for Tokyo to take his high school entrance exams, consoles the narrator for his loss. The hero's initiation is effectively postponed and in a sense universalized as he goes to sleep "warmed by the boy beside [him]" (p. 114), who of course faces his own initiation into school life away from his family.

The avoidance of direct total involvement in heterosexual love is not unique to this story, since most of Kawabata's central man-woman relationships do not build upon the mutual full engagement of two people. Frequently, his women are remote and virginal—"pure" as he sometimes calls them—and, whatever the author's psychological determinants for this may be,* there is a kind of aching persistent eroticism permeating his later novels which is inseparable from the wistful and often intense longing that typically marks Kawabata's male characters.

The atmosphere of freshness and innocence enveloping "The Izu Dancer" comes, I think, from Kawabata's utterly simple language which sets the experience down among the trees and clean air and wet grass of a country resort. In contrast to the urban environments of his Neo-Perceptionist works, the setting of this story recalls the province of the traditional *haiku*. There is also the circumstance that Kawabata, instead of explaining the characters' thoughts and feelings, merely suggests them by mentioning objects which, in a country setting, are certain to reverberate with tangible, if not identifiable, emotions.

> It was after midnight when I left their inn. The girls saw me to the door, and the little dancer turned my sandals so that I could step into them without twisting. She leaned out and gazed up at the clear sky. "Ah, the moon is up."
> (P. 112)

Here Kawabata, as he chisels this plain, clear prose reaching back to the old tradition, appears determined to find some alternative to the eccentric internationalism of his "modernist" stories.

Snow Country (*Yukiguni*) combines elements of Kawabata's Neo-Perceptionism with his *haiku* style of juxtaposition and understatement. The first thing that must be mentioned in this connection is the curious evolution of the work. In January 1935 Kawabata wrote two related short stories for different journals, "The Mirror of an Evening Scene" (*Yūgeshiki no Kagami*) and "The Mirror of a White Morning" (*Shiroi Asa no Kagami*).[6] Roughly corresponding to the first two sections of the final version

---

* Those with a psychological bent might consider his very early loss of both parents and grandparents as significant. Kawabata continually thought of himself as an "orphan." Also, in several works he quite candidly admits his adolescent homosexual experience.

of *Snow Country,* they were merely the start of that work, for in November and December 1935 two further related stories appeared, then two more in August and October 1936, and one more story in 1937, each in turn adding some development to the last published. All were then collected into a full-length work called *Snow Country* in 1937. But that is not all. In 1940 and 1941 he added still two more stories. The whole was revised some six years later, and it was actually not until December 1948 that Kawabata felt he was finally done with it.

What is extraordinary in this is of course Kawabata's free attitude about the wholeness and unity of a piece of literature. First, it took fourteen years for the story as a whole to be completed; second, the sections were published in different periodicals with little expectation that readers would have access to any section previously published; third, the final addition and revision, coming years after the earlier tentative completion, brought considerable changes in the text. All this seems to indicate that Kawabata had a sense of the novel as a temporally changeable entity built on the autonomy of each part. Clearly, the impact of such a fragmentary mode of publication on the form of the work as a whole is greater than, and different from, that of regular serialization. For instance, Kawabata most probably had no scheme at all at the beginning for any larger context. Each addition came as though it were the conclusion, implying no further future. And only much later, when he saw the possibility of a larger whole including what was already published did he begin to fit the new sections into this later conception. Such loose serialization allows also for adding to a work almost anytime if a larger scheme suggests itself. With a work of this sort, the search for "structural unity" is likely to end in one's grappling with the author's mere schematization, a ghost of the story, rather than with the energy and movement of the artist's spirit-quickening words. It is good to keep in mind here that while the imposed mode of publication may be prior to and thus determine the form of a work, the reverse could just as well be the case. That is, it is possible that Kawabata's particular temperament and artistic need actively sought out and chose this unusual mode of publication. Since he wrote so many other works, including *The Sound of the Mountain,* in this fashion, I am convinced that he knew what he wanted from serialization.*

Another way of getting at the situation is to stress the essentially temporal nature of Kawabata's art. Instead of spatially schematizing the continuity, planning a unique shape like a sculpture, Kawabata just lets his language flow in time, lets it weave its own strands, almost come what may. The "shape" of the novel is thus not architectural or sculptural, with a totality subsuming the parts, but musical in the sense of a continual movement generated by surprise and juxtaposition, intensification and relaxation, and the use of various rhythms and tempos. The *renga* form is often mentioned in connection with Kawabata and for good reason: it too is characterized by frequent surprises along the way and only the retrospective arrangement of the parts into a totality as they approach a possible end.

Snow Country recounts the love affair of a writer, Shimamura, with a resort geisha as it develops over a period of some twenty months during which he is intermittently a guest at a mountain spa. The story opens in the winter with Shimamura about to begin his second stay, but the sequence is interrupted shortly after his reunion with the geisha by a long flashback describing their first encounter the previous spring. After that, the story progresses in chronological order to the end, telling of the rest of his current stay and of a third visit the following fall. The seasonal order is thus from winter to spring, back to winter, then to fall which is

---

* Kawabata's explanation for publishing the first two sections in two different magazines in the same month is as follows: he couldn't finish the "Mirror of an Evening Scene" part before the deadline of one of the monthlies, so he decided to write the unfinished part for another with a later deadline. As he spent more time on it, his ideas about it changed.

Kawabata once called *Snow Country* a "work that could have been completed at any point." He said elsewhere, however, that he had wanted to include the fire scene "even while [he was] writing the earlier sections." As if to make the provisional nature of his structure still plainer, he also said that *Snow Country* might better have ended without the last sections—that is, those corresponding to the last 25 pages in Edward Seidensticker's translation (New York: Knopf, 1956), the edition used throughout my discussion. Kawabata's remarks are in Terada Tōru's article "Yukiguni nitsuite," reprinted in Mishima Yukio's collection of essays on the author (note 1).

passing slowly into winter. Not a complicated sequence, certainly, and yet the long flashback, together with numerous brief references to earlier events throughout the rest of the book, effectively disrupts the single sequentiality and thus creates a subtle sense of passing time. In fact, the persistent back-and-forth time motion is just confusing enough to lead the author himself into a miscalculation of the total time (three visits in "three years")[7] but the "error," not at all seriously misleading the reader, has the salutary effect of reinforcing the novel's diffuse sense of time's passage.

The flow of time which defines the shape of *Snow Country* is also an important thematic element, established at the very beginning by the celebrated mirror image. Shimamura struggles to remember the appearance of the girl he will soon see again. Only his tactile recall is strangely vivid: the forefinger of his left hand suddenly feels "damp from her touch." * In this frustrating state of sexual immediacy yet final remoteness of the loved one, he sees a woman's eye "float up before him." It is the reflection in the coach window of a girl sitting opposite him.

> In the depths of the mirror the evening landscape moved by, the mirror and the reflected figures like motion pictures superimposed one on the other. The figures and the background were unrelated, and yet the figures, transparent and intangible, and the background, dim in the gathering darkness, melted together into a sort of symbolic world not of this world. Particularly when a light out in the mountains shone in the center of the girl's face, Shimamura felt his chest rise at the inexpressible beauty of it. (P. 9)

* In the first printed version of this section, the word for "finger" was suppressed by the government, or by the publisher in fear of censorship. Though such deletion is irrelevant to the critical problem at hand, it does suggest an aspect of the modern Japanese novel which I have not touched on. The prewar and wartime censorship policy was codified into a dozen or more ruthless criminal laws ensuring the silencing of any "subversive" or "depraved" expression. Although the release from such repressive and puritanical censorship was celebrated briefly after August 1945, it was soon replaced by a number of regulations decreed by the American Occupation Forces which were almost as stringent in some respects.

The montage of the girl's face transparent over the continually moving landscape provides a good visualization of the book's main motif—the passage of time and man's continual struggle to slow it or pin it down to something substantial, or at least an image of something substantial. Shimamura, like anyone else, is continually compelled from the past to the present, and from here into the future, but he lives the present as though it were a somehow lasting extended stasis, the experience of beauty occasionally shocking the moving darkness into a radiant stillness.

Kawabata's handling of the mirror image is characteristically delicate. The reader is not let in on the full "symbolic" import of the superimposed image on the train window, and only after spending a considerable time with Shimamura is he allowed to discover—retrospectively as it were—that Yōko, the girl in the train window, is enmeshed in various relationships with Komako, Shimamura's geisha. The two girls complement each other to create the fullness of womanhood—one static, more timeless, less individualized (the name *Yōko* meaning "girl of leaves"); the other, dynamic and more fully alive in time (*Komako*, "girl like a colt"). Shimamura, as the reader discovers later, is attracted to both, but transient that he is, is capable only of observing them through the train window. Essentially a traveler, a passerby, he can only pass them by without becoming fully engaged with either of them.

Komako is one of very few life-sized and full-bodied female characters in Kawabata's novels. Uninhibitedly passionate, but she knows the futility of it all. She really loves Shimamura, but does not expect their relationship to proceed beyond a casual once-a-year arrangement. Time and again, she is described as "clean" or "pure" (*seiketsu*), as though she somehow embodied the crystal purity of the mountain snow. But at the same time, red is the color most often associated with her. Her character resonates on the poles of this oxymoron of purity and fire, carefully underlined by the mirror image at the beginning and the fire scene at the end. I find it remarkable that Kawabata is able to flesh out the logic of such a character into a real person, yet he does so, keeping her fire and ice somehow in balance. The other characters, principally Yōko and Shimamura, tend to be fainter embodiments. Against the boldly tactile realization of Komako, the intense and ethereal Yōko is hardly tangible. We are frequently told about her beautiful eyes, and her voice which seems to "come echoing back across the snowy nights" (pp. 5, 83). Yōko, thus disembodied, is the other half of a woman, the spirit or soul of a woman, always eluding men's reaching hands, always fragile and more than a little mysterious. Just as her voice seems an echo, her whole person appears not to belong to this world either. She is a fairy-tale figure, a symbolic marker, living not by her own will and desire but at the beck and call of the heroine— that is, to fulfill the logic of the drama.

Yōko's characterization deficits are thus fairly well justified by the central time-stasis paradox in the novel, but Shimamura's insubstantiality as a character is not so easily explained. Although the story is in the third person, it is told almost entirely from Shimamura's point of view. So much so, for instance, that the narrator does not even identify Komako by name until their reunion is fully told and a quarter of the story is well over (p. 51 of 175 pages). Thus, despite its third-person form, *Snow Country* is essentially a first-person novel. Similarly, if there is little distinction between character and narrator, neither is there much room between character and author. With "The Izu Dancer," a lyric inviting no ironic examination of the narrator's experience, this problem never arises. *Snow Country*, not being a lyric, calls for some critical investigation of Shimamura's point of view. Had this been provided, as in a dramatic monologue, we would have had clues to the author's stance toward the hero. As it is, the story remains disturbingly inconclusive in its judgment on its principal character.

Shimamura is an art critic. He is also the translator, supposedly, of "Valéry and Alain, and French treatises on the dance from the golden age of the Russian ballet" (p. 131). He writes articles and collects documents on Western dancers and productions although he has never seen a ballet, nor does he attend Japanese dance performances.

> Nothing could be more comfortable than writing about the
> ballet from books. A ballet he had never seen was an art

in another world. It was an unrivaled armchair reverie, a lyric from some paradise. He called his work research, but it was actually free, uncontrolled fantasy. He preferred not to savor the ballet in the flesh; rather he savored the phantasms of his own dancing imagination, called up by Western books and pictures. It was like being in love with someone he had never seen. But it was also true that Shimamura, with no real occupation, took some satisfaction from the fact that his occasional introductions to the occidental dance put him on the edge of the literary world —even while he was laughing at himself and his work. (P. 25)

This portrait of a self-ironic dilettante, a westernized intellectual who knows no ballet at first hand, no real West, indeed no real Japan, but who acknowledges his ignorance, even flaunts it. Such a portrait is uncomfortably close to one version at least of the self-image of the younger Kawabata himself. Note especially Shimamura's irony directed at both himself and his work, but more important, the total absence of irony operating on the portrait of Shimamura as a whole.*

Shimamura's behavior toward Komako, too, is left suspended finally in the novel's attitudinal limbo. Take the celebrated passage (pp. 146–47) where he tells her that she is a "good girl." Komako asks for some elaboration, and he repeats his remark, but with a variation: "you're a good woman." Many critics in discussing this change argue that Shimamura *inadvertently* reveals in his second remark his real attitude toward Komako as a mere sexual object. But there is no evidence for this. Besides being genuinely attracted to the girl, Shimamura is fully sensitive to the moral implications of his relationship. He knows he will never

---

* There are several literal-minded "scholarly" studies about the "real" setting and people that supposedly served as models. Kawabata himself has this to say about Shimamura: "I have remarked—in the Afterword to the Sōgensha edition of *Snow Country*—that 'Shimamura is of course not myself. . . . I am more Komako than Shimamura.' Probably that is correct, but it seems to me now that this is the kind of thing one cannot say decisively. Shimamura bothers me as the author of *Snow Country*. I would like to say that Shimamura is not really there, but even that is dubious." (Quoted by Terada Tōru, in Mishima's collection, p. 245.)

marry her and he feels some guilt about this, even if he never acts on it. There is overall a kind of neutrality in the book regarding Shimamura's character which a "moral" interpretation is bound to misrepresent.[8]

Despite the fact that *Snow Country* gives great prominence to the Tanabata legend, the scene of the starry heavens that concludes the novel is not clear enough in its significance to serve as a gloss on the work. According to the legend, Kengyū and Shokujo loved each other so much that God turned them into stars placed on either side of the Milky Way (conceived of in the myth as a river, Ama no Kawa). They are allowed to meet only once a year, on Tanabata, the evening of July 7, a holiday still widely observed by Japanese children. In the last scene of *Snow Country*, Shimamura, hurrying with Komako to watch a burning building, feels the "naked" Milky Way "wrap[ping] the night earth in its naked embrace" (p. 165);* the next moment it seems to flow "through his body to stand at the edges of the earth" (p. 168); and finally "the Milky Way flow[s] down inside him with a roar" (p. 175). The overwhelming galactic image here is very much like the rainbow in D. H. Lawrence's novel which operates as a symbol of promise of sexual fulfillment. The double message comes with the Kengyū-Shokujo reference which appears to emphasize the anguished separation of the lovers.

What I have come to believe is that Kawabata is ultimately indifferent to moral considerations in art. He will always, for instance, shift the narrative line so that the human action or situation is implicitly compared with a natural object or event which has in itself no single definite meaning at all, though it may be powerfully evocative of certain emotions. Take the passage describing the dying moth (pp. 89–90) or the one concerning the *kaya* grass (p. 92): they are there not so much to interpret and comment on the hero's action as to break the line of the story, or drop a hint that no matter what the characters may be up to, the

---

* It is unfortunate that the English equivalent of Ama no Kawa (literally, "River of Heaven") should be the "Milky Way" with its connotation of the breast and fecundity. Also, another name for it, Ginga ("Silver River"), has an association of coldness and clarity which most Japanese would automatically feel even in the name Ama no Kawa.

world around them is always present but uninvolved, insensible,
and not really attended to often enough. He reminds us to stop
and look. The kind of resigned sadness or loneliness one always
feels in Kawabata's novels comes, it seems to me, from his acceptance of man's helplessness before such a comprehensive flow
of things in time. It is not all sadness, of course, because Kawabata finds quiet pleasure in this acceptance.

Mishima's grasp of what Kawabata is about is correct in the
sense that he does not interpret the world as novelists are supposed to do. Yet he does interpret it. Time flows through the
process of his work, and he, having abandoned the effort to make
particular judgments all the time, sees men and women on a larger
canvas than human actions and their consequences can provide.
Kawabata sings the tune he picks up from the changing world
just as he hears it. In this way the acceptance of things as they
are becomes, in Kawabata's hands, a vital act of interpretation.

As we have seen from the discussion of the window-mirror and
the fire, *Snow Country* employs Neo-Perceptionist techniques
consciously distilled in the spirit of *haiku*. But there are numerous
other image-markers in the novel which act to animate and intensify the narrative movement. Such images at times approach
the gratuitous—Shimamura's visit to the town known for *chijimi*
linen (pp. 150–59), for instance, is not easy to justify without
forcing one's argument. Yet we can't help but see that the use of
the near irrelevancy is the strong new feature in Kawabata's art.

> The windows were still screened from the summer. A
> moth so still that it might have been glued there clung to
> one of the screens. Its feelers stood out like delicate wool,
> the color of cedar bark, and its wings, the length of a
> woman's finger, were a pale, almost diaphanous green.
> The ranges of mountains beyond were already autumn-red
> in the evening sun. That one spot of pale green struck him
> as oddly like the color of death. The fore and after wings
> overlapped to make a deeper green, and the wings flut-
> tered like thin pieces of paper in the autumn wind.
>
> Wondering if the moth was alive, Shimamura went over
> to the window and rubbed his finger over the inside of the

screen. The moth did not move. He struck at it with his fist, and it fell like a leaf from a tree, floating lightly up midway to the ground.

In front of the cedar grove opposite, dragonflies were bobbing about in countless swarms, like dandelion floss in the wind.

The river seemed to flow from the tips of the cedar branches.

He thought he would never tire of looking at the autumn flowers that spread a blanket of silver up the side of the mountain.

A White-Russian woman, a peddler, was sitting in the hallway when he came out of the bath. So you find them even in these mountains— He went for a closer look. (Pp. 89–90)

The kaleidoscopic succession of images—a dead moth, a cedar grove, dragonflies, dandelions, the river, silver flowers, a White Russian woman—effectively suspends the narrative progress and forces us to pay attention to those large margins in the canvas of life. Here, as in several other passages in *Snow Country*, Kawabata's use of one-sentence paragraphs strongly suggests the *haiku*, or the *renga*, a technique which will become a dominant feature of *The Sound of the Mountain*.

Overall, as compared with his earlier works, the verbal surface is more sedate in *Snow Country*, yet there are several residual experimentalist expressions. The opening sentences offer an example. In a literal translation, Ivan Morris puts it thus:

When [the train] emerged from the long tunnel at the provincial border, it was snow country. The bottom (or depth) of the night became white.[9]

Seidensticker gives this rendering:

The train came out of the long tunnel into the snow country. The earth lay white under the night sky. (P. 3)

There is another passage that is often talked about:

He leaned against the brazier, provided against the com-

ing of the snow season, and thought how unlikely it was
that he would come again once he had left. The innkeeper
had lent him an old Kyoto teakettle, skillfully inlaid in
silver with flowers and birds, and from it came the sound
of wind in the pines. He could make out two pine breezes,
as a matter of fact, a near one and a far one. Just beyond
the far breeze he heard faintly the tinkling of a bell. He
put his ear to the kettle and listened. Far away, where the
bell tinkled on, he suddenly saw Komako's feet, tripping
in time with bell. He drew back. The time had come to
leave. (P. 155)

For the bilingual, Seidensticker's excellent translation may seem
a little too clear, but the point is made very well for the English-
only reader. The metaphor of the wind in the pines is so intricately developed, changing to the sound of a bell, and then to
Komako's steps, that we can almost see Komako herself dancing
among the pines. The real and the fantasied are so closely woven
that we realize with a start that Komako's appearance is only in
Shimamura's consciousness. "The time had come to leave" is remarkably convincing as the reader is awakened from the reverie
he has been allowed to share. In the syntactically looser Japanese
version, the tenor and vehicle are even more subtly fused with the
effect of maximally blending the human movement into the occasions of Nature.

Snow Country essentially belongs to the prewar years, despite
the date of its final revision. (Other works written before and
during the war are: *The Flower Waltz* [*Hanna no Warutsu*, 1936],
The Master of Go [*Meijin*, 1942–54; translated into English in
1972], and a number of short stories.) During the time between
publication of the larger part of *Snow Country* and that of *The
Sound of the Mountain* falls, of course, the war, the single most
important event in modern Japanese history, and Kawabata is not
the kind of writer who could work comfortably under the increasing tension of those days. Unable to sift out his thoughts enough
to act politically, he was at the same time and for the same reason even less able to write. He spent this time reading deeply in

the Japanese classics—*The Tale of Genji, The Pillow Book, Hōjōki, Tsurezure Gusa*, Saikaku, Chikamatsu, and many *haiku* poets—and only gradually as his depression over the lost war and the lost national purpose slowly lifted did his pent-up creative energy begin to flow again. His postwar novels and novellas—*Thousand Cranes (Senba Zuru,* 1949–51), *The Sound of the Mountain (Yama no Oto,* 1949–54), *How Many Times, The Rainbow (Niji Ikutabi,* 1950–51), *The Dancer (Maihime,* 1950–51), *Days and Months (Hi mo Tsuki mo,* 1952–53), *The Lake (Mizuumi,* 1954–55), *To Be a Woman (Onna de Aru koto,* 1956–57), *House of the Sleeping Beauties (Nemureru Bijo,* 1960–61), and *Kyoto (Koto,* 1961–62)—were all published in the characteristic separate installments in different periodicals.[10]

What I have said about *Snow Country* also applies, in various ways, to many of these postwar novels. *The Sound of the Mountain* was published in seventeen sections in eight different periodicals over four and a half years (September 1949 to April 1954).[11] And again, each section is, to a large extent, autonomous, carrying a peculiar sense of completeness, yet open-endedness: for instance, had he decided in, say, April 1969 or July 1970 to add another section to *The Sound of the Mountain,* it need not have changed the novel materially. This non-Aristotelian aspect of his work must always be taken into account in any talk about Kawabata.

Once again, the flow of time that propels *The Sound of the Mountain* is inseparable from the substance of the novel. Written almost entirely from the point of view of Shingo, a man past sixty, it establishes at once that his memory of recent events is fast declining, while the people and events he recalls from the remoter past are becoming more and more vivid. As he shuttles back and forth between Tokyo and the suburbs, he remembers his home village, the girl he secretly loved there in his youth (his wife's older sister, long dead), and particularly the flaming maple tree she used to take care of. Against the general background of present dissolution, the remembered past offers him rest, solace, and solidity. But his life does have its present, too. More and more he sees the beautiful girl of the past in his daughter-in-law, Kikuko. If there is anything like a plot in the novel, then, it can be found commuting between these well-matched poles of the past and the present, death and life, with no perceptible advantage on either side.

Dissolution and death are everywhere around Shingo. His own marriage has for long lacked real warmth; his son, Shinichi, has a liaison with a war widow; Kikuko has an abortion in protest; his daughter leaves her husband, who soon thereafter attempts suicide with another woman; and his old friends die one by one of old age and the exhaustion of their struggle for survival in the difficult time after the war. Yet life rallies somehow. Shinichi and Kikuko begin to piece their marriage together again after he puts an end to his affair. Kinuko, Shinichi's woman, refuses to terminate her illegitimate pregnancy and fights to raise the child. Shingo's daughter Fusako, embittered and coarsened by her experience with her addict spouse and now probably a widow, nonetheless clings tenaciously to life.

If the balance of life and death has something to do with what *The Sound of the Mountain* is all about, the movement of the novel, its ever passing present, is also, paradoxically, a stasis, since it is all largely within Shingo's consciousness. The three locales—Kamakura (where the family resides), Tokyo (where Shingo and Shinichi work), and Shinshū (their country home) —function less as distinct settings than as spatial correlatives of Shingo's present and his past. More, even Shingo's workaday motions around Tokyo and Kamakura serve as occasions for reminiscence which set off at a moment's notice his reveries on long-lost things. Even the lesser characters are used at crucial moments mainly as prods to Shingo's memory: for instance, the novel begins with his asking his son to help him remember the housemaid's name.

Always at the center of Shingo's time-crossed consciousness is his daughter-in-law, Kikuko. She is his "window looking out of a gloomy house," * and he connects with the past and the present only through his love for her. His attachment is quite a different experience from an old man's purely erotic entanglement with a

---

* *The Sound of the Mountain,* trans. Edward G. Seidensticker (New York: Knopf, 1970), p. 37. This text is used throughout my discussion.

young woman, the kind Tanizaki Junichirō, for instance, so fondly describes.* Thus Shingo's many dreams all involve a degree of sexuality, but none of them unmistakably identifies the partner of his dream, nor do any of the dreams approximate real sexual union.[12] His erotic longing for his son's young wife appears to be powerfully restrained even on the unconscious level. Shingo fights against himself, continually "paternalizing" his attitude toward Kikuko. For union with Kikuko would be taboo in more than one sense: through Kikuko, Shingo reaches out not only to his wife's dead sister, but also to his own lost past. Kikuko is, in other words, much more Shingo's living memory standing before him than a living person. To abandon himself to his love for this young girl would be to surrender to the past, to a dead memory. His past must remain just out of touch, so he can live on in the shambles that the present is for him.

Kikuko is Kawabata's eternal untouchable woman, his Izu Dancer, his Yōko, exquisite and elusive. Once again we see that an approach to Kawabata's work in the expectation of meeting a fully realized female character is bound to be disappointed. Nor is Shingo, for that matter, a fully developed character. As is true of *Snow Country* and most other Kawabata novels, *The Sound of the Mountain* does not operate on ordinary novelistic logic. Rather, the play and performance of the images of things and their settings—whether related or unrelated to the characters— animate and move the novel. In the usual novel—here I have, say, Sōseki's *Light and Darkness* in mind rather than *Emma* or *The Ambassadors*—imagery serves mainly to reinforce the logic of the plot as it comments on the human drama. In *Light and Darkness* the night that envelops the hero toward the end—his dark night of the soul, as it were—suggests a crisis that might lead him to the "light" of self-knowledge. The image is there to amplify, intensify, and elaborate on the character's experience, not as it would be in *The Sound of the Mountain*, to dilute or deemphasize action. Of course, elsewhere in Kawabata's work, too, one

---

* In a sense, *House of the Sleeping Beauties* comes closest to Tanizaki territory. But Kawabata's eroticism is much more tenuous than Tanizaki's, the old man's contact with the sleeping girls merely setting off reveries in which he reminisces on his lost youth.

can find imagery that functions in this fashion. But *The Sound of the Mountain,* which is written for the most part in very brief paragraphs, moves at crucial points from image to image by a series of leaps. And these leaps are the novel's movement, the batteries that energize it.

The moon was bright.

One of his daughter-in-law's dresses was hanging outside, unpleasantly gray. Perhaps she had forgotten to take in her laundry, or perhaps she had left a sweat-soaked garment to take the dew of night.

A screeching of insects came from the garden. There were locusts on the trunk of the cherry tree to the left. He had not known that locusts could make such a rasping sound; but locusts indeed they were.

He wondered if locusts might sometimes be troubled with nightmares.

A locust flew in and lit on the skirt of the mosquito net. It made no sound as he picked it up.

"A mute." It would not be one of the locusts he had heard at the tree.

Lest it fly back in, attracted by the light, he threw it with all his strength toward the top of the tree. He felt nothing against his hand as he released it.

Gripping the shutter, he looked toward the tree. He could not tell whether the locust had lodged there or flown on. There was a vast depth to the moonlit night, stretching far on either side.

Though August had only begun, autumn insects were already singing.

He thought he could detect a dripping of dew from leaf to leaf.

Then he heard the sound of the mountain.

It was a windless night. The moon was near full, but in the moist, sultry air the fringe of trees that outlined the mountain was blurred. They were motionless, however.

Not a leaf on the fern by the veranda was stirring.

In these mountain recesses of Kamakura the sea could

sometimes be heard at night. Shingo wondered if he might
have heard the sound of the sea. But no—it was the mountain.

It was like wind, far away, but with a depth like a rum-
bling of the earth. Thinking that it might be in himself, a
ringing in his ears, Shingo shook his head.

The sound stopped, and he was suddenly afraid. A chill
passed over him, as if he had been notified that death was
approaching. He wanted to question himself, calmly and
deliberately, to ask whether it had been the sound of the
wind, the sound of the sea, or a sound in his ears. But he
had heard no such sound, he was sure. He had heard the
mountain.

It was as if a demon had passed, making the mountain
sound out.

The steep slope, wrapped in the damp shades of night,
was like a dark wall. So small a mound of a mountain, that
it was all in Shingo's garden; it was like an egg cut in half.

There were other mountains behind it and around it, but
the sound did seem to have come from that particular
mountain to the rear of Shingo's house.

Stars were shining through the trees at its crest. (Pp.
7–8)

Obviously, Shingo's experience is being described by the narrator
from Shingo's point of view. But it is not at all clear what this
litany of objects—the moon, Kikuko's dress, the locusts, the
sound of the mountain—and the precision with which they are
observed really amount to. Only free association of an aging man's
night thoughts? For that, the bright moon, the dress hanging on
the line, the screeching locusts and, of course, the sound of the
mountain have something too ominous about them. A direction
is being felt out, but where? The transitions between the very
autonomous paragraphs are disjointed (hardly any conjunctions
are used) and it seems that the sequences could stop at any time.
In fact, with each new paragraph, we feel a surprise, however
delicate, at still a new turn in the train of thought. It is not the
suddenness of a new percept that surprises, although the sound

of the mountain is indeed unexpected. "The moon was bright," "Though August had only begun," "Not a leaf on the fern," "Stars were shining"—the paragraphs, highlighting the objects of his consciousness, nonetheless gradually move away from the interior of his existence toward the container of all the drama—the world around, the wide margins of the novel.

As for Shingo's hearing the sound of the mountain, there is a mimetic aspect to it, certainly. First, the fact of his hearing the sound is stated unqualifiedly. Next, his causal inventory is given—windless night, nearly full moon, motionless trees, and the rustling leaves of the fern. Then, his more generalized question "If it is not the sound of the waves?" is answered, followed by a description of the sound as like "wind, far away." The next paragraph brings the question back to himself: isn't the sound coming from his own body? With his denial of every such possibility, the sound suddenly stops. Shingo is frightened. In this longest paragraph in the passage, he is said to "want to" ask the same questions again; that is to say, he can no longer ask since he already knows the answers. The fearfulness of the experience is underlined by the reference to the "demon." [13] Thus, Shingo's psychological reality is available to us here: an aging man's fear of death by some inexplicable and possibly diabolical natural event. And yet the attractiveness of the passage does not depend entirely on the mere representation of the old man's state of mind. The man and his presence approach transparency as we begin almost to hear *through* Shingo the ominous sound of the mountain. Shingo himself is not really very substantial in this moonlit reality; rather it is his instrumental role in making accessible the wide world that spreads around him. For Shingo, as for Kawabata, the awareness of the large margins of the world around human beings and their actions, the large area of silence that stays intact despite human speech and the words of the novel—that is what powerfully informs his mind.

Shingo is no Leopold Bloom, whose stature and massive weight can carry the burden of everyman everywhere, in the whole city of Dublin and beyond. Mrs. Dalloway—or Mrs. Moore, for that matter—might be a closer analogy, with her delicacy and apparent fragility. But as a character Mrs. Dalloway has a rich and substantial interior life; she has angst and terror and tenderness, frivolity and sensuality, and an overall self-awareness embracing both her past and her present. Shingo as a character shies away from such definition, and it is only his remarkable sensitivity that identifies the context of his personality within the novel.

Kawabata's achievement, it seems to me, lies in just this, his keen awareness of the objects around men that exist in themselves as solidly as people do. Objects, in the world and in the world of the novel, are somehow or other related to people, but Kawabata seldom makes the connection between them explicit for us. With each of his brief paragraphs self-contained in this way (and, I should perhaps add, with each of the brief installments also self-enclosed), these objects tend to stand autonomous. Although he continually invites us to make our own efforts to connect, he stops short of giving us the keys to the house.

> Far distant flow of time. White chalk. The picture of a flower on the blackboard at a girls' high school. A brief life, a girl. A white sail on the horizon. The crystal in the eyes of a fried fish served at a hotel. Near-sighted fish; oh, poor fish. A gynecologist's instrument looking like a fork. ("The Crystal Fantasy," *Complete Works,* II, 195)

What I would call Kawabata's nominal imagination is apparent even in his earliest work. The objects here are not organized syntactically. He does not relate them, with verbs and conjunctions, into a sentence, a proposition, but just leaves them as he finds them. Exactly in the same way, *The Sound of the Mountain* reaches out and gathers objects into a narrative, but refuses to hook them into a chain of cause and effect, a plot.* They are

---

* Kawabata wrote a book on the theory of the novel, *Studies of the Novel* (*Shōsetsu no Kenkyū*) (Tokyo: Kaname Shobō, 1953), which is not on the whole very interesting to those who already know James, Lubbock, Forster, etc., whom Kawabata considerably simplifies in his discussion. However, his brief discussion of plot is of note, largely because he complains here about the lack of a well-constructed plot in Japanese novels. He argues that the Japanese writer regards fiction as somewhat against the "laws of nature," and even in writing a novel he wants to follow nature as it is: like the *haiku* and the *waka,* the novel rejects falsification and, together with it, the carefully constructed plot (pp. 44–50). Kawabata also published a collection of essays on prose style, *Bunshō* (Tokyo: Tōhō Shobō,

assembled but unconnected. What emerges, then, is not an argument—which any construction of plot (the whole cause-effect complex) implies—but a perception of the world and an acceptance of it as perceived, one thing at a time. It is a world parceled and scattered in a way more ruthlessly than even the broken family and society in *The Sound of the Mountain* can justly reflect. Yet even while referring to the myriad objects in the margins of human existence, Kawabata manages to be happy in the radiant beauty he finds there.

Kawabata's art is always immediately recognizable. As Ivan Morris and others have pointed out, it is finally traceable to the traditional sensibility of sadness (*aware*) over the transience of men and things, as exemplified by Lady Murasaki, Sei Shōnagon, and countless other writers and poets. As such, it is not easy to talk about in modern critical terms, as Mishima's incomplete statement seems to imply it is. What is so convincing to me about Kawabata's art is the vibrant silence about it; the delicate strength in the leap of images, and finally, in his refusal to connect things into an easy meaning, his embrace of the shambled world. The lack of "structure," often mentioned as though it were a blight on his work, is Kawabata's way of adjusting the novel to the flow of time so that art can survive and teach men and women to survive.

Kawabata's suicide in the spring of 1972 surprised people. There were many speculations: his shock at his friend Mishima's *harakiri*, his overexposure since winning the Nobel prize in 1968, his general exhaustion and sense of decline, and—correlative no doubt to all these—his dependence on barbiturates. Now, a little later, with the gossip quieted, if not stilled, the self-administered death begins to look more accidental than essential. Because with Kawabata, there is no evidence in his art of any compulsion toward this end. His writing did not derive from his personal life in the way Dazai's or Mishima's did and thus reach a dead end following a life-decline. He had a way too of always clearly know-

1942), certain of which are fascinating in their discussion of children's writings in comparison with "literary" works.

ing the risks of the artist's life, and knowing the measures to take to avoid them. All his life he managed to keep up a working détente between his art and his life and the terrible demands of both by always closely attending to what I have chosen to call the margins of life. His suicide terminated his life no less abruptly than Dazai's or Mishima's, but the feeling is inescapable that it was something almost natural in Kawabata's case, an easier and gentler crossing than theirs had been. And all the more difficult, then, to resist the seductiveness of death. For Kawabata, the margins of life blend imperceptibly into that yawning voiceless world and are finally commensurate with it.

V

TILL DEATH DO US PART

DAZAI OSAMU: *The Setting Sun*
—Forgive me that I was born.

People loved Dazai. Friends and hangers-on were always
around him, recording his slightest gesture and memorizing his
utterances as if they were prematurely preparing hagiographies
on the master. For all his liberal handouts of cash and drinks, it
really was him they seemed to require. This sardonic clown, gen-
erous and compassionate to a fault, was at the same time selfish
and perverse to a greater fault. For many adorers, he was a decadent saint, tireless in his search for the grounds of belief. For
other acquaintances, he was a fool and a loser, whose embarrassing self-consciousness disabled him from forming any decent
product out of the bathos of his life. Japanese critics writing on
Dazai are unanimous in seeing real talent in his rare sensitivity
for language. His friends and disciples, however, seldom write
about his works; instead, notes, personal memoirs, books like
*Dazai Osamu: His Life, Dazai Osamu the Man, Dazai Osamu's
Charms,* and *Seven Years with Dazai Osamu* pour out every year,
and now there is even a periodical called *Dazai Osamu Studies.*[1]
Young people modeled themselves after him, to the extent of com-
mitting suicide with a copy of a Dazai clutched close. He was an
institution of postwar Japan—until the catapulting prosperity of
the sixties skipped over the traces of those wretched years.

Dazai lovers look for the man in his works, and there is good reason: he is less open to consideration apart from his work than any other writer discussed in this book. There is a monomaniacal "first-person" quality about everything he wrote. No matter what mask he assumed, it is always his own, very personal self who is speaking. He wrote everything furthermore with the expectation that his reader would recognize and enjoy *his* words, *his* thoughts, *his* feelings. For him a novel was a personal record, and its fictionality consisted in its tonal manipulations, the various ways he looked at himself. The seer was Dazai, and the landscape Dazai, and despite the high degree of tonal variation, Dazai always believed he was being absolutely honest. Fiction was the "truth" for him, that is, non-fiction—a paradox that shows itself whenever a Dazai is read.

First, then, to the "truth"—those facts of his life which he felt compelled to review and report time and again throughout his career. Dazai Osamu (1909–1948) was born Tsushima Shūji, the tenth of eleven children of a rich, locally powerful landlord in a small town in the north. In that part of Japan at that time, to be one of the younger sons in such a home meant relative neglect by the parents. Worse still, his father, a member of the House of Peers, died when Dazai was only fourteen. Dazai was sent away to school in a nearby town, and it was there he made his first suicide attempt. Around this time he came to know a young geisha, Koyama Hatsuyo, whom he eventually invited to live with him when he entered the French Department of the University of Tokyo in 1930. His eldest brother, now head of the family, intervened and Dazai was forced to send the girl home. A few months later, he tried to drown himself with a cafe waitress, whom he had known only two weeks. The girl died, Dazai survived. Charges of abetting a suicide were brought against him but were quietly dropped. A few months later he finally managed to get together again with Hatsuyo, though at the cost of formal severance from his family. Active for a while in support of communist causes, he gave up his underground activities upon learning that Hatsuyo was not a virgin at the time of their marriage. I am not quite sure what the connection might be between one's politics and one's wife's premarital experience, but that is Dazai's explanation

for his "conversion" (*tenkō*) and surrender to the police in 1932.[2]
In the meantime he had dropped out of school as well, unable to
master the first lessons in French.

Only gradually, as he began to publish some short stories in
magazines, did he become serious about his writing. Chaos persisted in his life. In 1935 he tried to hang himself after failing to
get a newspaper job. By now addicted to morphine, he was sent
away several times for withdrawal and treatment. Returning from
one such cure, he was told by Hatsuyo about her adultery during
his absence. He attempted suicide again—this time with Hatsuyo
—but neither died. They separated, however, and the next year he
married a quiet high-school teacher. Legally, at least, the marriage
lasted till his death.

Dazai remained prolific throughout his *Sturm und Drang*, and
by the time he was in his late twenties his work began to attract
wider attention. Japan was on the eve of the Pacific War, and
writers were censored by the war policy-makers on grounds of
subversion, depravity, or irrelevance. Then when the American
air raids intensified, both his home in Tokyo and his wife's in the
country (to which he had moved) were bombed out. Toward the
end of the war and into the postwar period, he wrote for Tokyo
newspapers and magazines from his parents' home in the north.

He returned to Tokyo in late 1946 appearing frantic to burn
out whatever was still uncharred in his life—talent, energy, life
itself. He earned money only to throw it away on alcohol and
women. By this time seriously ill with tuberculosis, he nonetheless
wrote, drank heavily, and got involved with women, all in utter
indifference to his health. One woman, a young war widow, sent
him her manuscripts for advice. Later she asked him to father a
child for her. He complied. The affair went on for a while and then
he came to know another war widow, a former hairdresser, whose
apartment he began to use occasionally for writing. And so it
went, until it was all over on the day—it was his thirty-ninth
birthday—they found his body tied by a cord to that of the devoted former hairdresser in a rain-swollen stream near his home.
The novel he was currently serializing was called "Good-Bye"
(*Gutto Bai*).[3]

So much for the "facts" of his life. Take any segment of the chronology, and you will find it amplified and "fictionalized" in at least one of his works, often in several. The central events are repeated in slightly different form in many stories: there is, for instance, his tragic-comic "marriage" to Hasuyo which is told in several versions, ranging from the fairly factual "Eight Scenes of Tokyo" (*Tokyo Hakkei,* 1941), using real names, to the more imaginary *No Longer Human* (*Ningen Shikkaku,* 1948). Not that this "truth" should be compared to a more "objective" version of it based on external evidence. Simply, one should recognize the habit of Dazai's imagination to fold back continually on his own life and feed on it.

The earliest collection of his stories, published in 1936, was called *The Declining Years* (*Bannen*). Dazai apparently meant by the title that his end was already present at the beginning, which is true: the book's most conspicuous features precisely forecast those of his later works. First, there is the absence of a coherent unity. Even as short stories, the items in the volume are fragmentary. There are a few meant to be collections in turn of shorter units, these having, however, no evident common denominator among them. For instance, the very first item, called "Leaves" (*Ha*), is no more than a few dozen aphorisms and paragraphs which at times string out to something of a story. Second, the "first-person" quality of Dazai's work is fully present in his first book. I do not necessarily mean here the use of the pronoun "I" specifically, although it is indeed prominent. Rather, the first person is implicit even in stories employing dramatic personae.* "The Monkey-Masked Clown" (*Sarumen Kanja*), for

---

* "Autobiographical" is the word I am deliberately avoiding here. *David Copperfield, The Mill on the Floss, Sons and Lovers,* and *A Portrait of the Artist* are all usually called "autobiographical," but the difference is that in these books the authors have managed to provide their surrogate characters with emotions and thoughts to some extent independent of the authors' own by taking a more or less clearly discernible stance vis-à-vis the characters. The fact that "events" in their works often derive from their own experience is, finally, not very important when considered in the context of the works themselves. Dazai's "first person" is in a sense *meta*-autobiographical: the "I" is insufficiently filled out to constitute a truly independent character in the book, and thus so much is left to the reader's assumed knowledge of the writer himself. This is true even of a work written and

one, maintains an ostensible third-person framework, insisting on the presence of a would-be writer distinct from Dazai Osamu. But the mask is admittedly transparent. In the first paragraph, "this man" is said to have a "habit of thinking of himself as a 'he' "— as though the "he-ness" had no "reality." Dazai soon seems uneasy with even this thinnest of masks, and before long he abandons it by turning the story of "this man" into a series of letters which are not only first person, but no longer pretend to be "in character." The requisites for a complex narrative manipulation are all there. With Dazai, however, his apparent preference for vocal complexity derives less from his overall artistic plan than from his serious unease in the discipline of maintaining an even fictional distance from his work.

Concomitant with this is the author's preoccupation with the "truth" of his life which is boldly evident in "Recollections" (*Omoide*) describing the childhood of an "I" identical with Dazai. But the almost compulsive confessionalism is prominent even in supposedly fictional pieces like "The Paper Crane" (*Kami no Tsuru*), which describes the "I's" extortion from his wife of a confession about her premarital experiences, and his reaction to the revelation. The whole story enclosed in quotation marks, "The Paper Crane" is to be taken as a letter addressed to a "you" who is a fellow writer. More concerned with the speaker's own reaction than with either the wife's act of confession or her premarital life itself, the story quickly becomes the speaker's confession, and it is *his* urge to confess and show himself that energizes the work. Clearly, the confessor's presence is vital, but the story also maintains the structure of a double listener: the "I" who receives his wife's "truth" and the "you" (or reader) to whom his own confession is addressed. The final effect of the story thus very much depends on the reader's willingness to accept the intimate role of a "you" who is a kind of father-confessor for the speaker. If he is inclined to feel friendly toward the "I," he will like the story; if not, he will be bored by it.

---

read during his relative obscurity. Although many Japanese writers and critics tend to identify this type of first-person work or I-novel (*shi-shōsetsu*) with the post-Renaissance individualism of the West, the two traditions are really quite different.

Dazai's movement in "The Paper Crane" from the relatively simple form of a confession to that of a confession about a confession is part of the larger pattern of involution in his writing. The "I" in "The Paper Crane" is a writer who writes about himself as a writer. He also writes to a writer. Such an imaginative realm is bound to be self-enclosed. Where unable to penetrate the boundary of the self even a little, Dazai's imagination must forever turn back on itself. His self-consciousness is a series of Chinese boxes, endlessly reduplicating themselves. His work talks about his work, which talks about his work, which . . . Formally, we can see how this is related both to confessionalism and to the tendency toward division and subdivision in his work. The involutionary substance of his work is also inseparable from his habit of authorial intrusion. Dazai is not interested in sustaining a certain level of fictionality in his work, which would mean wrenching himself away from the self and constructing a separate world. That would be a lie. Fiction is a lie, and he must be honest at all costs. So he breaks in at points with a new intimate revelation, disrupting whatever fictional order exists. He is a cannibal, his compulsion to nullify the distance from his work—and from his reader—amounting to eating them up and eating himself up. Fiction is after all a trivial matter, while his hold on himself is of vital importance to him. But if his self-digestion must stop somewhere, it should be at the innermost core of the self, where there is possibly some resistive substance that will stand revealed in art, in spite of art.

If Dazai's art were no more than a cloak of rags to be torn away to disclose the truth, his work would prove quite tedious at the end, being merely the redundant self-analysis of a seedy self-indulgent individual. Such, fortunately, is not the case. Unlike the run of the mill "I-novelists," Dazai is remarkably versatile in varying his tones. The subject may be the self-same "I," but he is looked at variously from a wide range of angles including a self-ironic braggadocio, a sly mischievousness, and an immovable depression. In "Leaves," for instance, there is a quote from Verlaine attached to the title: "The ecstasy and the agony of being select, I have them both." From such Romantic stridency, he moves on to the insouciance of the first aphorism:

I thought of suicide. Last January I was given a present, a piece of fabric for a kimono. The material was linen, woven in narrow grey stripes. It is for a summer kimono. I thought I would live until summer.

The funny second one breaks the mood nicely:

It occurred to Nora [of *A Doll's House*], too. It occurred to her when she got out to the hallway and slammed the door. Shall I go back?

Thus we are invited to join the author on bright days and dark nights along the wayward progress of the work. And since the characters in his work, being essentially inseparable from the author himself, grow up and age along with the author, over the years we get to know him as though he were an old friend whose whole past is continually open before us. Rather than being confined to any specific work, Dazai's art transpires over the long period of time and the numerous works shared by author and reader.*

Dazai wrote a great deal, filling the twelve volumes of his *Complete Works*[4] during a mere dozen years after 1935, the most interesting "Dazaistic" works appearing in the postwar period, his last three years. Most of his works are characteristically brief; some, medium length ("The Flower of Clowning," 1935; "Das Gemeine" [his title], 1935; "The Spring of Fiction," 1936; "Human Lost" [his title], 1937; "Eight Tokyo Scenes," 1941; "The Sound of the Hammer," 1947; "Villon's Wife," 1947), and several, book-size (*The New Hamlet*, 1941; *Justice and Smile*, 1942; *Lord Sanetomo*, 1943; *Pandora's Box*, 1946; *The Setting Sun*, 1947; and *No Longer Human*, 1948).

---

* I agree to a large extent here with Howard Hibbett's articles, "The Portrait of the Artist in Japanese Fiction," *Far Eastern Quarterly*, XIV (May, 1955), 347–54, and "Tradition and Trauma in the Contemporary Japanese Novel," *Daedalus*, XCV (Fall, 1966), 925–41. Hibbett's tracing of the *shi-shōsetsu* back to the old "wayward essay" (*zuihitsu*) is, I think, the correct one. Only, I would like to add that the sensibility (*fūryū, aware,* and so forth) energizing the *zuihitsu* imagination is no longer available to modern writers. Although some residual attitudes are certainly to be found in their work, the old sensibility is hardly ever of much help in a real spiritual crisis.

The "first-person" quality is relentless in these works. Its simplest manifestation is Dazai's occasional use of his own name in the middle of a "story" (as in "Das Gemeine"), ever threatening to transform it into a kind of familiar essay. There are also frequent references to his earlier works (to *The Wandering in Fiction* in "A Small Album," and to "Human Lost" in "The Brazen Face," to name only a couple) and the occasional introduction of an old character (Ōniwa Yōzō of "The Flower of Clowning" in *No Longer Human*), both of which tend to open up a larger context of intimacy with the reader, complemented by Dazai's habit of directly addressing him. Other first-person features are the predominance of diary and letter forms in his work and the use of the dramatic monologue.

The diary form comes to Dazai almost effortlessly. "Human Lost," written in November 1936, covers the "I's" life in October and November of that year, referring at one point to his stay at a mental hospital very much like the one Dazai himself retired to at this time for treatment of his drug dependency, and, at another, to his relationship with his wife, identical to Dazai's and Hatsuyo's. As with all diaries, this one begins and ends with the start and finish of the duration of time covered, and there is little organizing impulse arising out of the work itself. Its "fictionality" depends almost entirely on the degree of one's ignorance about the author: a reader who knows nothing about the author's life might be impressed by the "inventiveness" of the situation and the "imaginative" arrangement of the characters, and respond positively to its various verbal and stylistic features such as the recurring waves of pathos, the *haiku*-like disjunction, the rhythm of involvement and detachment, and indeed the aura of confidentiality inherent in the form itself. Of course the better-informed reader will tend to consider first the generic aspect of the diary form and make some comparisons between the real or imagined private "truth" of the author and the public "fiction" of his work. Such a reader will be prepared to admire—or not—the author's insight into a situation in which he, the author, was in fact involved. A human being's life experience and his response to it are what constitute the work, not some severed self-enclosed imaginary experience. Among Dazai's diary-form works, even the more fictional ones like *Justice and Smile* (*Seigi to Bishō*) arouse similar reactions, depending on the reader's information.

The letter form occasionally poses similar problems, when as in *Pandora's Box* (*Pandora no Hako*) at least some of the letters composing the work are slightly altered versions of the author's actual correspondence. When these personal letters are addressed to the generic "you," as they often are, the reader's role as confessor is quite explicitly set. Of course, there are letter stories with distinct personae for both writer and addressee, and in these works Dazai can be quite successful in striking a balance between truth and fiction. After all, the epistolary form permits the author to invest his thought and feeling in the letter-writer, while enabling him to stand at the critical distance implied by the identified addressee. "The Sound of the Hammer," for instance, describes the writer's recurrent hearing of a hammer striking, which inexplicably drums down whatever energy and interest he might feel at crucial moments of his life. All the defeated man's gloom and despair is gathered into the dry, hollow sound of the hammer, while Dazai's self-ironic awareness is expressed in the comment on the letter attached at the end.

For this reason, too, the dramatic monologue is Dazai's most natural métier. While it allows him to commit his ideas and emotions to the assumed persona, it also leaves room for critical irony. Unlike Browning, Dazai always treats his speaker gently, never stooping to undercut him with too poisonous an irony (as can be found in "My Last Duchess" or "The Bishop Orders His Tomb"). Humor and mischievousness best fit a sensibility like Dazai's; he can straddle the fence, lampooning and pleading at the same time. "Villon's Wife" (*Viron no Tsuma*), for instance, is a woman's apology for her abusive writer-husband. By creating a speaker who is a sympathetic victim of his surrogate, Dazai can simultaneously plead for understanding from his reader and project a fair degree of ironic judgment on the whole matter. Thus by balancing his distress and his critical intelligence, he can go as far out of the self as he ever can for an outside view.

To be sure, Dazai's works are not all "first person." There are some that try to be "third person." Among the most conspicuous are his renderings of old well-known works. Dazai's fictional imagination, seldom sustained enough to fabricate a whole tale, requires some ready-made lifelike material if his own life is not to be used. So he reinterprets and reevaluates *Hamlet*, the life of a samurai hero, an obscure German play (translated by Mori Ōgai), various pieces from folklore and fairy tales. But even here, the plays and tales he whimsically remodels are fascinating—we see *his* imprint everywhere—while the works he took seriously, like *The New Hamlet* (*Shin Hamuretto*) and *Lord Sanetomo* (*Udaijin Sanetomo*), are almost unreadable. The reason is obvious: works having their own existence forced an examination on their own terms before they would submit to a rewriting. Clearly Dazai was a thoroughly first-person writer.

Dazai's first-person techniques are best utilized in three of his last and best works, "Villon's Wife," *The Setting Sun,* and *No Longer Human* (*Ningen Shikkaku*), which are the climax, and the conclusion, of his writing career. Since Dazai himself, as I read the modern Japanese novel, constitutes both climax and conclusion of the I-novel tradition, a closer examination of the best known of these novels is in order.

The Setting Sun (*Shayō*) was completed in June 1947 and serialized in a monthly magazine from July to October of that year. Dazai thus had no numerous deadlines to fight, and this novel is consequently somewhat more of a piece than his other long works. But fragmentation, of course, is the inescapable shape of his vision, and this work, too, inevitably breaks up into diaries, letters, and confessions, with all that such first-person forms imply.

The story is told by a young divorcée, Kazuko, born to a declining aristocratic family and now living with her old, ailing mother in a small country villa. When Kazuko's younger brother, Naoji, a war veteran and an addict, comes home, he is chaotic and depressed, upsetting his mother and sister by his wild habits. Having once wanted to be a writer, he still hangs around with his old teacher, an alcoholic named Uehara, who earns drinking money by writing. After the mother's death, Kazuko decides to have a baby by Uehara, who once kissed her on an impulse. Thus one day when Naoji comes to the house with a bar-girl in tow, she slips out to visit Uehara and asks him to make love to her. She returns

home to find Naoji has killed himself. The novel ends with Kazuko's letter to Uehara announcing her hoped-for pregnancy.

The characters and many episodes of *The Setting Sun* undoubtedly have their sources in Dazai's personal life. The two
writers, the aspirant Naoji and the fast deteriorating Uehara, are
impersonations of Dazai himself. The central event, Uehara's
fathering a baby for Kazuko, is of course Dazai's experience.
Dazai's family, if not precisely "aristocratic," was old enough
and once rich enough to make many people attribute that status
to it. Narcotics usage played a considerable role in the author's
life, and the depression permeating the novel closely resembles
Dazai's. To the extent that Kazuko makes excuses for both Naoji
and Uehara (as Villon's wife does for her husband), the novel
becomes Dazai's self-apology. Thus, what we have here in *The
Setting Sun* is the *shi-shōsetsu* par excellence—in its imaginative
energy, as well as the events, characters, setting, and tonality.

The one element of the novel which does not entirely succumb
to the prevailing death-wish is the heroine Kazuko herself. But
even at that, she is scarcely brought to life in the novel, being
little more than a half-hearted rekindling of the author's by then
almost smothered life-force. Indeed, her quasi-immaculate conception, like so many Biblical references in Dazai, sits there rather
isolated, without significant integration with the rest of the work.[5]
And there are other elements of the novel deriving from extra-
personal sources that also fail to cohere with the rest. One is the
running reference to *The Cherry Orchard*. Thematically, Chek-
hov's play of course treats the decline of the aristocracy, but beyond this thin resemblance, there is no reasonable basis of comparison between the play and the novel.[6] Another is the snake
imagery that appears at the death of both parents. Regardless of
the reptiles' possible psychogenetic origin, they are not adequately
shaped into a significant artistic role in the book. For instance,
there is Kazuko's disposal of the snake eggs, a snake's appearance
at her father's deathbed, the snakes' "mourning" in the garden
at his death, the "delicate, graceful" mother snake's search for
her lost eggs, and then the by-then expected appearance of a snake
at the mother's deathbed—all these episodes seem to carry some
elaborate symbolic significance, but they fall far short of making

it clear and become merely props for the scenery of impending death.

If there is one "idea" dominating the novel, it is Dazai's notion of "aristocracy." On the first page Kazuko quotes her brother's opinion: "Just because a person has a title doesn't make him an aristocrat. Some people are great aristocrats who have no other title than the one that nature has bestowed on them, and others like us, who have nothing but titles, are closer to being pariahs than aristocrats. . . . Mama is the only one in our family." [7] Later she refers to her mother as "the last [noble] lady in Japan" (p. 135; my restoration). And Naoji's "Testament" ends with the sentence, "I am an aristocrat" (p. 181; I omit "after all"). Aristocracy in this context is not merely the equivalent of a class title or birthright, but is a spiritual achievement. Alas, what constitutes such attainment is nowhere made clear in the book, since the characterization of those persons styled "aristocrats" is not full enough to bear analysis. Kazuko's mother, for instance, possessed of gracious table manners and free-spirited enough to pee in the garden under the full moon, is also stoical enough to keep smiling regardless, never be mean, always be considerate, and always be cheerful. But do such attributes make an "aristocrat"—a noblewoman, an elect? Nowhere in the novel is this titled lady allowed to be a full character, with her own thoughts and feelings, and the reader can see in her only her children's wistful longing for some distinction in their lives, for which no clearer definition or formula is provided than Dazai's global concept of "aristocracy."

As for Naoji's being an "aristocrat" there is even a larger question. The novel twice presents Naoji in his own words, once from his notebook and again from his will. "The Moon Flower Journal" is a series of aphorisms the Dazai reader has long been accustomed to:

Philosophy? Lies. Principles? Lies. Ideals? Lies. Order? Lies. Sincerity? Truth? Purity? All lies. (P. 66)

When I pretended to be precocious, people started the rumor that I was precocious. When I acted like an idler, rumor had it I was an idler. When I pretended I couldn't write a novel, people said I couldn't write. When I acted

like a liar, they called me a liar. When I acted like a rich
man, they started the rumor I was rich. When I feigned
indifference, they classed me as the indifferent type. But
when I inadvertently groaned because I was really in pain,
they started the rumor that I was faking suffering.

The world is out of joint.

Doesn't that mean in effect that I have no choice but
suicide?

In spite of suffering, at the thought that I was sure to
end up by killing myself, I cried aloud and burst into
tears. (Pp. 70–71)

His last note is more of the same, the fact that it is addressed to
Kazuko only slightly differentiating the tone from that of the
supposedly readerless diary:

I wanted to become coarse, to be strong—no, brutal. I
thought that was the only way I could qualify myself as a
"friend of the people." Liquor was not enough. [I had to
be perpetually in the whirlpool of dizziness.] That was
why I had no choice but to take to drugs. I had to forget
my family. I had to oppose my father's blood. I had to
reject my mother's gentleness. I had to be cold to my
sister. I thought that otherwise I would not be able to
secure an admission ticket for the rooms of the people.
(P. 166)[8]

Beneath the debauchée's mask, the note asserts, Naoji conceals a
noble spirit and some tender feelings. Maybe. But the reader
finds in this supposedly final revelation nothing to substantiate
his claim. It contains in fact little besides self-pity and an over-
acquaintance with exhaustion and defeat: he cannot cope with
life, so must choose death. Now, a capacity for stylish suffering
may be the sine qua non of the elect, but that alone does not suf-
fice. As Dazai himself recognized in his quotation from Verlaine
in his very first publication, what is also needed is the intelligence
to understand the despair and the strength to transform it into
the joy of life. Naoji's death-wish is perfectly understandable—

his life does seem wretched enough. But the death-wish alone cannot admit one to the aristocracy.

One has to question why Dazai felt he had to revive the notion of aristocracy anyway, especially in those postwar years when so much of the legal and hereditary hierarchy was being dismantled. Of course, "class" might reasonably survive and even flourish in a vertical society such as Japan's, suddenly leveled in the early postwar period by starvation, worthless yen, and the U.S. occupation policy. But even more to the point, perhaps, is the author's own quasi-aristocratic background. That he was an "aristocrat" is usually taken for granted by the largely middle-class Japanese critics,[9] who also believe that his underground politics in the 1930s and his lifelong rebellion against various authority figures (father, eldest brother, the state, teachers, the literary establishment) had a common origin in his guilt for having been high born.[10] But there is something unauthentic about Dazai's so-called high birth. Rich and powerful the Tsushimas may have been, yet they do not belong to the families of feudal lords (*daimyō*) or courtiers (*kuge*). Dazai was brought up like any other small-town middle-class child of the 1920s. For instance, he attended regular public schools (not the Peers' School and College—the Gaku-shūin), and he had no firsthand knowledge whatsoever of the Japanese aristocracy, which was a very exclusive club indeed in prewar days. It is no exaggeration to say that Dazai's upper-class identification was more dream than reality. True, among radicals he may have felt a little sheepish about his landlord father and comfortable upbringing, and yet can't we see this "guilt" as at least in part a sneaky regret for not *really* belonging to the actual aristocracy, which alone could presumably license for him some genuine guilt about his background, in the style of a new Hamlet or a latter-day Lord Sanetomo?

The lie can be accounted for in several ways. During the Meiji era writers, as we saw in chapter 1, had considerable difficulty locating the right level of reverence for the narrator. Should he look up to his reader or talk down to him? Is he primarily teacher or entertainer? Since that time, the Japanese novelist has studied the West and learned about the serious role of the artist in modern

society as well as certain things about the Western art of novel
writing. But exactly what constitutes the artist and his "voice"
has never been satisfactorily decided: he is neither a poet-philoso-
pher who speaks for the whole nation, such as Balzac and George
Eliot wished they could be, nor an alienated critic like Proust or
Joyce who speaks for a select few. Surely he is a *sensei*, a master.
But what does he teach? Except for a few like Kawabata, most
Japanese writers had to fall back on the old Confucian notion of
the master respected not primarily for his craft but for his knowledge, experience, and wisdom. Dazai too wrote from the assigned
position of a wise teacher documenting his learning and experience
even while totally rejecting the conventional morality. It is on
such insights, well hidden behind the cloak of depravity, that the
"aristocratic" label should be pinned. As a decadent rebel, however, Dazai discovered early in the game that his peerage would
not be recognized by the philistines at large, whose support he
certainly needed, especially in his moments of loneliness. It is at
this point that he made the imaginary leap from the fictional (but
in a way real) claim to selection by achievement to the literal (but
fake) claim to selection by birth. Very much like Oscar Wilde's
double-edged paradox of fiction and reality, this complicated manipulation of fact and fabrication must have had enormous appeal
for Dazai the "soothsayer."

Still there is a confusion inherent in the notion of "aristocracy"
in *The Setting Sun* which I see as inseparable from Dazai's child-
like uncertainty about the whole social milieu and how to relate
to it. He defied authorities all his life, but he was also invariably
in awe of them. There are many stories about his hankering for
acceptance, of which his desperate wish for the Akutagawa prize,
a kind of Japanese Pulitzer prize, is only one example.* And he
was never able to resolve conflicting impulses in relating to others.
He fared better with those socially beneath him, but even then he

---

* When Dazai's "The Flower of Clowning" was nominated for the newly created
Akutagawa prize in 1935, he pestered his sponsor Satō Haruo to fight for the
prize for him. Satō records his annoyance at Dazai's greed in his "Akutagawa Shō,"
collected in Koyama Kiyoshi's *Dazai Osamu Kenkyū* (Toyko: Chikuma Shobō,
1956), pp. 397–415. Incidentally, one of the judges voting for one of Dazai's rivals
was Kawabata Yasunari.

was no Whitmanesque prophet of the streets. Only with his youthful admirers does he seem to have felt truly at ease.

In a vertical society, a person with no developed sense of his own place, one who cannot "size up" at once his relative position of superiority or inferiority with anyone he comes into contact with, is lost. He will not even be able to conduct a comfortable conversation with anyone except a close friend. If he happens to be a writer, the results might very well be disastrous. For the novel, unlike poetry, must define a character within an actual society; the writer must locate his sympathy or hostility on the social map so that he may set out the novel's scenes, shape its plot, and populate its world. And this is exactly what Dazai was unable to do. Those early radical activities of his notwithstanding, he soon became wholly indifferent to political problems; despite his frequent references to Marxism and the Revolution, his social and political understanding did not go beyond the level of the average high-school student. True, Dazai was an uncomfortable person, and he felt vague sentiments for social justice. But he possessed neither an analytic mind nor adequate knowledge of his society to do anything about it. *The Setting Sun* is not only vague in its notion of aristocracy; it also lacks sufficient scale and the sort of developed attitude toward its society that would provide a powerful and comprehensive vision of postwar Japan.

And yet we recall that the book was wildly popular around 1950, contributing the word *shayō-zoku* (the people of the setting sun) to the nation's vocabulary. Besides, Dazai accomplished something no other writer could do in recent Japan—he brought colloquialism back to the written language.

In the multiple-leveled Japanese language, Dazai's awkwardness in finding the correct social position for himself in the pyramid parallels his inability to find the correct level of reverence in speech. It should be remembered here that the system of honorifics is, as we saw in chapter 1, not a level of politeness, and not "cultured speech." It is a whole involved process of minutely adjusting one's every utterance to conform to tacitly assumed relative positions among speaker, listener, and referent. However distasteful one may find this assumption of hierarchy—although very few Japanese would readily challenge *the* first principle of their so-

ciety—there is simply no easy way out of the linguistic constric-
tion. A neutral level exists only in the artificially created area of
official announcements and technical writing, and nowhere in
ordinary speech situations involving speaker, listener, and referent. Even more difficult to learn is the art of silence—the highest
decorum in Japanese culture—whereby the socially inferior expresses deference to his superior by the shut mouth, not speaking
at all. Expression, even of respect, is often a rude assertion of the
self that is rejected by those who hold firm to the tradition of the
language and its value. Dazai, however, at once rebel and philis-
tine in language as in life, could neither commit himself fully to
the system of honorifics nor abandon it entirely. Use of a formal
and correct Japanese employing subtle gradations of hierarchy
would place him as a member of the fold, which he is not; a rough
and slangy Japanese overriding precise gradations would make
him a churlish schoolboy, which he also is not—besides, even the
most vulgar speech is never free from implied caste. Thus, as in
social intercourse, Dazai is always slightly bewildered, slightly
fidgety where Japanese is concerned. And this speech embarrassment, part and parcel of his social awkwardness, is powerfully
operative in the making of his style. For instance, no one is more
sensitive than Dazai to the possibility that any mode of speech
may turn absurd. Whenever his writing turns a bit too ponderous,
or affected, or cumbersome, or rigid, or just too formal, he shifts
into reverse and writes with humor, or a meticulously measured
colloquialism, or vulgarisms, or babyish onomatopoeia, or a
sprinkling of learned diction and foreign words, here and there a
grotesque word, an archaism or two, or he omits a pronoun or a
postposition, or he staccatos a passage with overpunctuation. Occasionally, especially in the aphoristic diary pieces, he can somehow manage to stay neutral, but even there his remarkable awareness of the ever-possible absurdity keeps his style clear of the
turgid and the affected alike.

Those who know Japanese sense this at once, although I am
aware of how hard it is to convey the sense of it to those who
don't know the language. What Edward Seidensticker meant
when he called Dazai a "poet" [11] is at least partly this quality, I
believe. And I regret that discussion of the precise dynamics of

one language is extremely difficult to conduct in another. The translations of the works are of little help sometimes in getting across this "poetic" quality. Donald Keene's version of *The Setting Sun,* for example, though generally excellent, fails at times to transmit the nuances of the rude and the polite in Dazai's writing that makes his style dance with such rare grace. I can only point to the drunken chant at Uehara's party, "Guillotine, Guillotine, shooshooshoo" (p. 147), or the old mother's use of the word *oshikko* (wee-wee) as bringing in just the right touch of absurdity to the respective passages which, by a sort of juxtaposition and reversal, set in motion waves of rich connotation. Probably Dazai's most notable stylistic accomplishment lies in his creation of that pervasive feeling of shyness and embarrassment in his work, reflecting the overwhelming absurdity he so purely perceived all around him. The gap between the spoken and the written language is still a very serious problem for the Japanese writer, and Dazai managed to show at least one direction for a possible coming together of the two.

The "I-novel" reaches a dead end once the author's life is completely exposed. After that, further writing risks a redundancy which is nauseating for the writer himself as well as for his reader.* Then his imagination must get to work inventing new experiences to write about. The rewriting of older works, *Hamlet* for Dazai or *The Tale of Genji* for Tanizaki, may afford temporary relief, but when that has been tried, unless the writer's psychic makeup is extraordinarily vigorous, like Tanizaki's, he will not have much to do except tackle the one experience no one has ever personally reported on—death. Thus the *shi-shōsetsu* writer is never free of the temptation of suicide. Dazai's four fail-

---

* Deliverance from the cursed *shi-shōsetsu* maze is certainly not by way of "polished style," as many Japanese critics seem to believe. Shiga Naoya, for instance, whose scorn of Dazai drove the author to almost hysterical fury (as expressed in "Thus Have I Heard" [*Nyoze Gabun*], 1948), is as much a victim of the whole convention as Dazai himself. Shiga's extraordinary failure of self-criticism is repugnant to any critical reader, and yet, quite surprisingly, his smug self-portrait, *Through the Dark Night* (*An'ya Kōro*) (1921–37), is quite widely hailed as a masterpiece by Japanese readers—with the exception of a few such as Nakamura Mitsuo. See his *Sakka Ron* (Tokyo: Kōdansha, 1957), I, 10–139, esp. 83–89.

ures at death were in a way requirements of his art. His fifth attempt, the successful one, was also required.* The *shi-shōsetsu*, by its own logic, will not close until the writer's life closes. And Dazai himself had to bring it to its conclusion. If Naoji and Kazuko and Uehara are "victims," so is Dazai a victim—of the Japanese novel, of the Japanese language.

---

* Some biographers believe that Dazai did not really want to take his own life, but was forced into the double suicide by his companion. While this is not impossible, there seems to be little hard evidence for it. Besides, whatever may have been the immediate circumstances of his suicide, Dazai's lifelong will to death is hard to deny.

Shocked at Mishima's death, several critics wrote about suicide and Japanese writers. Yoshida Seiichi, in his article "Bungakusha no Jisatsu to Mishima no Shi," *Gunzō*, XXVI (February, 1971), 205–11, chronicles about thirty suicides by writers just since the Meiji era. His list does not pretend to be all inclusive, of course. In a special issue of *Kokubungaku: Kaishaku to Kanshō* (December, 1971) entitled *The Writer and Suicide (Sakka to Jisatsu)*, Ōhara Kenshirō (editor of the issue) points out that the suicide rate for Japanese writers is "three hundred times higher than that for Japanese men as a whole" (p. 18). Although Ōhara's evidence for his figure is necessarily quite flimsy (who is a "writer," for instance?), there is no question but that the suicide rate for Japanese novelists, poets, intellectuals, freelancers, pulp writers, and so on is extremely high. For further discussion of this see chapter 6, on Mishima.

VI

MUTE'S RAGE

MISHIMA YUKIO: *Confessions of a Mask*
and *The Temple of the Golden Pavilion*
—*Nothingness was the very structure of this beauty.*

The shocking harakiri was called for by the shooting-star course of his life. This most talented and spirited of the postwar Japanese novelists produced over thirty novels, scores of plays, and numerous essays and pamphlets totaling well over a hundred volumes.[1] Yet he also found time and vitality to practice *kendō* and *karate*, weight-lifting, and other body-building exercises, to sing, model, act in films, organize his own army and design its uniforms, get married, stay married, travel, run with the jet set, and entertain lavishly. There were hints along the way, particularly during the last several of his impatient forty-five years, when there appeared a kind of frenzy in his life, though we know from his well-known bursts of uninhibited laughter that he stayed courteous and full of fun and self-irony. Mishima had also read the world's literature exceptionally well, from Euripides to Witold Gombrowicz, and Japanese works from *Kojiki* to unknown new writers, and in his own life he would allow not the slightest hint of any misidentification of book and life. Indeed, he often expressed unqualified contempt for men like Dazai who had supremely confused the two. Referring to the *shi-shōsetsu* writer, he asked, "Why do some Japanese writers feel the curious impulse to become characters in fiction?" [2] He wanted his characters to speak for themselves, not for their author. Yet, for all that determination, there is a strange still point just beneath the dizzying whirl of words and gestures, the silent decibel of an ever-present horror.

The horror is discernible even in his analytic writing about fiction. Mishima wrote a great deal about the novel, and one of his most serious discussions is a long, incomplete essay, "What Is the Novel?" (*Shōsetsu towa Nanika*), which was being serialized at the time of his death. Here he categorizes fiction (as against the quasi-fiction of the historical novel, the I-novel, the documentary novel) as "having a conclusive finality in language expression" (meaning, no further reference beyond language) and as "belonging to a dimension totally different from that of facts, no matter how much resemblance to facts the objects and events within a work may have." [3]

This direction in Mishima's thoughts about fictional language says something about the complex organization of his imagination. For instance, referring to the need for right naming, he says that, faced with the job of naming, in fiction, any object little known to the general reader, the novelist feels he has three choices. Take the problem of naming something like the obscure type of door known in Japanese architecture as the "Maira door": the writer can explain it without giving it a specific name ("the door, often seen in old homes, that has many horizontal crosspieces"), or he can coin a descriptive phrase ("the horizontal-crosspiece door"), or he can use the right name while sneaking in an explanation ("Maira door, is that the name?, the door with many horizontal crosspieces"). Mishima's method is still another, to name it by its right name, leaving to the uninformed reader the job of finding what exactly the name refers to. Of the three substitute expressions, the first is unsatisfactory because, while the writer is observing the object correctly, he is not at all earnest about locating the right name; the second, coining an expression, is irresponsible because, quite simply, no such expression exists; the third, however, is the worst. Mishima dislikes this the most because the writer, though vaguely aware of the accepted name, is shifting responsibility for confirming its accuracy onto either the character or the reader. The writer is not committed to language, and this attitude of indecision and hanging back is grafted onto the character as well.

There is a good deal to be said in favor of his argument. Somewhat reminiscent of Ezra Pound's principle of "ching ming" (true naming), Mishima's essentially conservative insistence on the use of the right name for a thing is salutary in view of the chaos of neologisms and loan words of the modern Japanese vocabulary. At the same time, there are two notable unclarities, which might reveal something important about his fictional stance but which are never resolved here.

First, Mishima's notion of a "conclusive finality of language expression" ("language is all") is not argued thoroughly enough. Does he mean that "meaning" in fiction is determined solely by the context of the work without further reference to the outside world? If this is so, shouldn't we say that the differences among the four names for "Maira door"—the right name and three spurious "names"—constitute different meanings? Why this puristic attitude that one "right name" alone can assure fictional autonomy, regardless of context?

Second—and this is surprising—Mishima consciously and assertively takes a stand against letting characters choose their own language, regardless of dramatic necessity: "It is an annoying wrongheadedness to make use of a deliberate pretension of ignorance for the purpose of expressing the character's carelessness." That is, every word written in fiction reflects only the author's own judgment, and not the character's. In its final sense, this is of course true of any literary work, but that is not what Mishima means here: when his characters are allowed to speak, their language must always be their author's. All expressions must be "accurate" in the sense of "correct," "right," or "authentic." And, although this statement may explain Mishima's usually orthodox and decorous style, it points at the same time to an essential contradiction between his practice and his often pronounced belief in objectivity.

It seems, then, that what Mishima means to stress by insisting on the autonomy and finality of expression is not so much the ontological independence of a work from both author and subject matter as a sort of finish or hard-polished surface which in actuality may have very little to do with the sought-for "objectivity" in a work of art.

The essay includes an analysis of his last work, *The Sea of Fertility*, the third volume of which had just been completed, and here Mishima returns to the question of the autonomy of fiction. He talks about the uncertain future awaiting both the tetralogy and himself, but goes on to say this does not mean that "the future world of the work itself and the future of the real world will ever merge and mix, just like the parallel lines in a non-Euclidian mathematics. . . . The future of the work is already potentially there in the two thousand sheets so far written, and its future will not be able to avoid the inherent inevitability. It is inconceivable that the end of the future world of the work and the end of the real world will perfectly coincide in time." This insistence on the essential separation of art and life is of course gratuitous: no one questions that the two will never meet. And yet he must emphatically reiterate it. "When Balzac was sick," he remembers, "he had to cry for a doctor out of his own work. Writers often confuse the two realities. For me, though, the most essential methodology in art and life has been never to confuse them. . . . For me, the fundamental impulse for writing is born from the contrast and tension between the two realities." The expression "contrast and tension" is ambiguous enough; with a slight shift in emphasis, the meaning could almost be reversed:

> I cannot think of the world after the end of this work; I hate and fear to imagine that world. When these floating realities finally part, one to be discarded and the other to be sealed into a work, what will happen to my freedom? . . . Unless the reality outside my work forcefully carries me away, I will someday fall into deep despair—though I am fully prepared for it. To come to think of it, I was even in my childhood always waiting for a disaster that might never come. . . . And that childhood habit still continues, turning me into a writer who cannot work without the sense of crisis coming from the contrast and tension between the two realities.[4]

Life and art must be kept separate, but the "contrast and tension" between them intensify to an unbearable pitch as they hopelessly mingle and threaten to merge. In the subtle dialectic of Mishima's imagination, the face and the masks, life's reality and art's, are forcibly separated, and yet they continually move together. The "objectivity" of his fiction is itself but one more mask, and rather a transparent one at that. How absurdly appropriate, then, that the date of completion, November 25, 1970, attached to the end of the last volume of the tetralogy, his final and most ambitious work, should be the day he chose to end his life.

Mishima Yukio, or Hiraoka Kimitake (or Kōi), the oldest son of an upper-echelon civil servant, was born in Tokyo in 1925. Though remotely connected with the last generation of the Tokugawa shogunate family, the Hiraoka family had no claim to a title. Despite this, they had some pretensions to aristocracy: Mishima's given name, for instance, means "princely dignity." And his parents felt their son should be educated at the Peers' School and College (Gakushūin), which until the end of the war was an institution belonging to the Imperial Household and devoted largely to the proper education of the royal scions and the children of the aristocracy. He was a sickly child, but he did well in the school. At his graduation, he was cited by the Emperor for the highest achievement in his class. He began to write while still in his teens and adopted his pen name soon afterward. Although he graduated in law from the University of Tokyo and worked briefly in a promising post in the Ministry of Finance, he resigned from his job in 1948 on the strength of a score of short stories published in various journals. He was just twenty-three years old, but from the beginning of his writing career, he had the knack of making just the right contact at the right time in the closely knit Tokyo literary world, and his rise was dazzling.

The early works are not very good. Mishima's first volume, *The Forest in Full Bloom* (*Hanazakari no Mori,* 1944), is a collection of precociously decadent and detachedly romantic stories, many of which recollect a colorful but boring upper-class life long gone even then. Also they provide a heavy dose of nationalistic rhetoric glorifying the beauty and elegance of the Imperial past

—a fact interesting in view of their author's later works. The elaborate and archaic vocabulary and general aloofness to the drab and wretched scenes of wartime Japan similarly foreshadow his mature works, whose motifs, images, and themes are already apparent. With *Confessions of a Mask* (*Kamen no Kokuhaku*), published in a single volume in 1949, Mishima entered the forefront of the Tokyo literati.

The book is divided into four chapters of varying length. The account of the protagonist's relationship with Sonoko lasting for some four years occupies the second half, while his development up to the late teens constitutes the first. Overall, the progress of the plot follows the protagonist's growing-up years with no temporal disruption. Structurally, however, there is no clear beginning, middle, and end, nor is the division into four marked by any discernible stages. It is notable, too, that the narrative tempo slackens considerably as the work proceeds.

In the earliest part, the "I's" memory is spotty. At the opening, we are told of a rim of light he remembers from his own birthscene, reflected from the edge of the round basin in which he had his first bath. The story quickly turns to his survival, at the age of five, of a near fatal illness caused, we are told casually between dashes, by autointoxication. Without dwelling on the possible meaning of such spots of time and experience, he hurries on to an account of how as a child he was inexplicably excited by such things as the sight of a nightsoil man, the smell of soldiers' sweat, or a picture of Joan of Arc. The references are all in quick succession in the first ten pages with little analysis from the narrator. As the "I's" self-awareness develops, there is an increase in frequency of more analytic comments which connect the episodes. Also, as he grows older and the distance between experiencing self and narrating self diminishes, the narrator begins to concentrate on his sexual impulses, which focus alternately on Sonoko and his own body. There is now a full analytic commentary on each episode, retarding the passage of time and intensifying self-consciousness. The change in narrative style of course underlines the changes that occur between childhood and youth, in the perception of time and the self, but more importantly it dictates a change in the modality of the work from that of a highly imagistic, "poetic" narration to a more novelistic one. The gain in psychological fullness appears to be at the expense of lyrical intensity.

Since the term "lyrical" presupposes subjectivity and privacy, what is the significance of the title, "confessions of a mask"? How confessional is the work, and what is the mask?

It is undeniable that Mishima makes full use of the material of his personal life. The "I's" family, education, induction, and job experiences, even his life-chronology parallel Mishima's own, even to the extent that the "I's" first name, "Kō-chan," mentioned a few times, is a common diminutive of Mishima's real first name. There seem to be only a few deliberate alterations of details, such as his father's first name. As for the dominant circumstances of the work, the narrator's sexual inversion and his relationship with Sonoko, there is no reason to believe either that they are literally true, or that they fall completely outside the author's experience. Although I am not thoroughly familiar with the biographical details of Mishima's youth, nor am I aware that a good study of his early years as yet even exists, autoeroticism and homosexuality themes do appear continually in his works, some of the scenes from this novel recurring elsewhere in almost identical form. Presumably, too, Mishima's pursuits in later years—his military games and relentless practice of body-building exercises, for instance—also confirm his main sexual orientation. Thus there is little question that the narrated life and Mishima's personal experience do conform at least in outline.

But to locate such a correspondence between life and art need not mean that *Confessions of a Mask* is a personal account. For justifying the paradox, we need only refer to the truism that *any* literary work, even if intentionally "autobiographical," is always fictional, since it is bound to select and arrange, and hence interpret. Mishima's is an even more daring gesture, as though the purpose of his "confession" were solely to mock the Japanese literary preoccupation with the personal I-novel. There is evidence here of a calculated aura of exposure meant to deflate the slightest suspicion of dishonesty; and there also appears to be a determination to "show the worst" so that possible charges against it of fictionality, deception, and hypocrisy may be dismissed once for all. The bull (of the I-novel) is thus taken by the horns (of honesty and truth). And once successfully released in this way from the clutches of confessionalism, he would be free to tell his story, which is a fictive form despite its use of nonfictive facts, circumstances, and truths. Those who want to know the inner and outer reality of Hiraoka Kimitake's personal life will learn very little from the book. The character of the "I" is surprisingly flat and volumeless, as I would like to show later.*

Confessions of a Mask is in the first person. Obviously, the narrated self merges into the narrator at the end where both are a young man in his early twenties. But even at the very beginning the distance between the two is not really noticeable. Unlike the mature Pip recalling the young Pip, the narrator takes no advantage of the great ironic possibilities inherent in age and experience distancing. One reason may be that the narrator himself is still a young man and thus not so "distant" from the scene after all. But there is something more to it than that. Just as the imaging in the earlier parts is of such a striking clarity, the immediacy of the narrator's recall of his earliest days is also remarkable. Thus, instead of an older man interpreting as he presents his younger self, this younger self is essentially one with a still-young narrator. For this effect, the loose tense of the Japanese is highly successful. The narrator's story is often in the present tense, which essentially obscures the distinction between time past and time present.

---

* *Confessions of a Mask* is obviously susceptible to psychoanalytic interpretation. Its bizarre fantasies (especially the Saint Sebastian image, and the dream fantasy of cooking a live friend, stabbing a fork into his heart, and slicing his flesh), together with the narcissism and inversion themes, clearly invite such treatment. There is one psychoanalytic study called *Mishima Yukio niokeru Nanshoku to Tennōsei* by Yamasaki Masao (Tokyo: Guraffiku-sha, 1971), but its argument is both unscrupulous and unintelligent. There is also a publication giving Mishima's Rorschach responses and their analysis by Kataguchi Yasushi, but I have not been able as yet to obtain it. In the "Writer and Suicide" issue of *Kokubungaku: Kaishaku to Kanshō* (December, 1971), Hasegawa Izumi gives a biographical sketch that is as of now the fullest account of Mishima's life. His father, Hiraoka Azusa, has published a memoir, *Segare, Mishima Yukio* (Tokyo: Bungei Shunjū, 1972); it is quite incoherent and contains little information. An American article tracing the bloody images throughout Mishima's works, "Greek Hero and Japanese Samurai: Mishima's New Aesthetic," by Gwenn R. Boardman, *Critique*, XII (1970), 103–113, while not specifically Freudian, is suggestive.

Where this happens, the narrative sequence following the "I's" chronology does not easily yield a thoroughgoing consequentiality which arranges events into a plot, nor does it suggest an overall connected meaning. The power of the work arises instead from intensity and concentration of feeling. In this sense, *Confessions of a Mask* takes rather the form of a lyric than of a novel.*

What then is this feeling that focuses the narrative? We may consider some possibilities. Is it the narrator's agonized isolation resulting from his knowledge of his sexual inversion? His recognition of the gap between ought and is? His despair over the conflict between homosexual impulses and his determination to be fully heterosexual? Or, the obverse of such awareness, an utter narcissism? Perhaps they are all represented in the book, and yet we sense they are finally a little irrelevant. The "feeling" I am talking about here is not particularly the "I's," but our own feeling aroused as we read. The "I" in fact is amazingly devoid of most normal feelings; it is almost as if he had set out to eliminate from the narrative any trace of an emotion he might once have felt. Take his relations with his family: he never records his emotional responses to them. When his sister dies, at the beginning of chapter 4, he remarks how he "derived a superficial peace of mind from the discovery that even [he] could shed tears." [5] How are we to take this? Should we be impressed by his toughness? Or tacitly grant that he has some tender brotherly feelings under that mask of indifference? Or is it possible that the writer is sitting on the

---

* One might recall here some of Virginia Woolf's works, although her "lyrical novels" like *Mrs. Dalloway* and *To the Lighthouse* are informed by a rigorous time-sense.

In "My Wandering Years" (*Watakushi no Henreki Jidai,* 1961), collected in a book with the same title (Tokyo: Kōdansha, 1964), Mishima, talking about the background of the *Confessions,* maintains that "ignorance as youth's privilege" is an idea "suitable for poetry, but not for the novel," adding that even so he "tried to force it into the novel form" (p. 42). He made several assertions elsewhere regarding the "un-autobiographical" nature of the work. Toward the end of his life, however, in remarks on the *Confessions* during his interview with Akiyama Shun—in *Taidan: Watakushi no Bungaku,* ed. Akiyama Shun (Tokyo: Kōdansha, 1969), p. 88—he seems to have admitted that it reflected his actual feelings during much of his adolescence.

fence, striking a pose for both effects, while not really knowing for sure what sort of sensibility he should give his character? *

Of the more important relationships in the book, take that of the "I" and Ōmi. Clearly, he loves Ōmi as he does nobody else. But to say that is to say that Ōmi arouses him sexually as does no other friend (we leave aside all the soldiers and laborers the very sight and smell of whom has excited him since childhood). Ōmi is beautiful, strong, and rebellious. But his character qualities do not matter much; it is his appearance—his body—that arouses the narrator. It is as if the adored Saint Sebastian had stepped right out of the Guido Reni painting and stood before him. If the "I's" passion here is genuine, it is also exclusively physical. And Ōmi isn't even aware of it, as the Saint Sebastian in the picture would not be either. Actually there is hardly any reciprocal feeling between the two. If there is on the narrator's part a sort of painful groping for Ōmi, it should not be confused with a striving for Ōmi's love or approval, for his expectations exclude all but the hardest sexual pleasures, which he can, after all, indulge all by himself. There is the lovely scene of the early morning after a snowstorm, where the "I" follows a set of fresh footprints with the vague feeling they may be Ōmi's, until they spell Ōmi's name and the "I" and his friend stand face to face. For a moment, there is just a hint that the "I" may be encountering someone as lonely and fearful as himself: "The instant I had seen that enormous OMI drawn in the snow, I had understood, perhaps half-unconsciously, all the nooks and corners of his loneliness—understood also the real motive, probably not clearly understood even by himself, that brought him to school this early in the morning . . ." (p. 60). But that is not the way the "I" meets Ōmi or anybody else. Ōmi, boyishly shy and awkward, thrusts his leather gloves against the cheeks of the "I," whose reaction is "a raw carnal

---

* In a short-story essay, "Chair" (*Isu*, 1951), Mishima describes his relationship with his mother and grandmother in greater detail, although even here the narrative voice stays detached and ironic. *Selected Works* (see note 2), X, 65–80. At the same time, in a short essay called "The Departure from the Feeling of an End" (*Shūmatsukan kara no Shuppatsu*), his actual feelings on his sister's death are described as violent. He writes that he loved his sister almost incomprehensibly, and that he totally broke down when she died. *Collected Essays* (see note k), p. 416.

feeling" that blazes up within him (p. 61). Sympathy and ir-
ritability, intimacy and self-defensiveness, affection and hatred
—such impure combinations of feelings that muddle and enrich
human intercourse are almost totally alien to the "I," who
chooses to keep his crystal-clear sexual image of Ōmi and his own
specific sexual response free of all such ambiguities. Thus, once
Ōmi is expelled from school (only about thirty pages after he
first appears in the story), he promptly ceases to exist for the
"I." There is, for this young man, no silly missing his friend, no
indulgent dwelling on the past.

Sonoko's entry into the *Confessions* is preceded by the sound
of her piano practice which the "I" overhears while visiting her
brother. (The piano music motif recurs later on in the *Confessions* when the "I" tries to pick up their relationship again after
her marriage.) Thus *Sonoko* is of sound, as Ōmi is of images. In
this sense, as sound penetrates more deeply than the visual image,
Sonoko is ready from the beginning to move more deeply into
his consciousness than Ōmi can. Here then there may be more
likelihood of some reciprocity. But does it happen really?

The narrator is moved by her innocent beauty. Under the
threat of war and all its dangers, they are drawn to each other.
But can he love her? He begins to feel that for a fulfilled life he
must be close to Sonoko, but can he develop real feelings of
pleasure in sexual contact with her? He wonders, and Sonoko
thus becomes a test by which he might prove his heterosexuality.
Her family leaves Tokyo for the duration, and he visits her in the
country. Their courtship now assumed by her family, he feels
he must conduct the final test. When he kisses her and feels no
pleasure whatever, he at once concludes he can never love her.

They break off but he meets her again after her marriage, and
they resume the relationship. On one of their rendezvous he takes
her to a dance hall, only to find his attention drawn irresistibly
to the nude perspiring torso of a young laborer.

> At this sight, above all at the sight of the peony tattooed
> on his hard chest, I was beset by sexual desire. My fervent
> gaze was fixed upon that rough and savage, but incom-
> parably beautiful body. Its owner was laughing there un-

der the sun. When he threw back his head I could see his thick, muscular neck. A strange shudder ran through my innermost heart. I could no longer take my eyes off him.

I had forgotten Sonoko's existence. I was thinking of but one thing: Of his going out onto the streets of high summer just as he was, half-naked, and getting into a fight with a rival gang. Of a sharp dagger cutting through that belly-band, piercing that torso. Of that soiled belly-band beautifully dyed with blood. Of his gory corpse being put on an improvised stretcher, made of a window shutter, and brought back here. (P. 252)

Sonoko has to go home at that point, and as the "I" stands up, now fully realizing what he is and what he is not, what he can be and what he cannot be, his eye catches the puddle of a spilt drink "throwing back glittering, threatening reflections" from the table (p. 254). We may recall the bright rim of light he remembers from his birth-scene.

Even from this brief outline of their relationship, one can see how the story is centered on the narrator himself, and how it ignores her side entirely, dismissing even her response to him. Just as Ōmi was no more than a part of his fantasy, Sonoko, too, is merely an aspect of his self-experiment. She will do as he dictates. If she cannot arouse him, she is of no use to him and he must leave her. If there is any discomfort on his part, it is not over the injustice to Sonoko, but related solely to his realization of his "destiny." Throughout the book, there is only the "I" who feels and does not feel, thinking about himself, looking at himself. This "I" fills the whole story, leaving no room for anybody else. Where then does the intense lyricism, the almost moving sadness, come from?

There is nothing about narcissism which is essentially antithetical to lyricism. Some of Wordsworth's poems are just as self-centered as the *Confessions,* if not more so. But even in egotism, Wordsworth knew how to let himself go and move toward otherness, often in doing so lifting the weight of the mere self to the height of sublimity. With Mishima, however, the narrator seldom lets himself go with his powerful emotions. As soon as they are registered, loneliness and despair—or joy and pleasure on a few occasions—are intelligently outlined and effectively dealt with. For instance, when still a further test of his heterosexuality fails —he visits a whore with a friend—he describes this reaction:

> I assumed that my friend had no suspicion of what had happened, and surprisingly enough, during the next few days I surrendered myself to the drab feelings of conva- lescence. I was like a person who has been suffering an unknown disease in an agony of fear: just learning the name of his disease, even though it is an incurable one, gives him a surprising feeling of temporary relief. He knows well, though, that the relief is only temporary. Moreover, in his heart he foresees a still more inescapable hopelessness, which, by its very nature, will give a more permanent feeling of relief. I too had probably come to expect a blow that it would be even more impossible to parry, or to say it another way, a more inescapable feeling of relief. (Pp. 226–27)

The paradox seems to sustain him for a while. Then, his friend lets him know he knows.

> My cursed visitors finally left at eleven o'clock, and I shut myself up for a sleepless night in my room. I cried sobbingly until at last those visions reeking with blood came to comfort me. And I surrendered myself to them, to those deplorably brutal visions, my most intimate friends. (P. 228)

Where even his visions are part of a rational plan, there would seem to be little room for lyricism.

In this book of confessions in which almost everything is taken note of and accounted for, there is one thing the narrator leaves largely unanalyzed, and this is the gradual change in the attitude of the "I" toward his self-understanding. In the first chapter the story is wholly episodic, and the "I" understands, in his own way, what he is doing. But he is never self-conscious about his mode of self-understanding. His reaction to the nightsoil man and other physical workers; his fascination with the picture of a knight on a white horse (ending abruptly when he is told the knight is a

woman); his excitement at smelling soldiers' sweat; his early
transvestitism; his sadistic rewriting of Andersen's "Nightingale";
his war games with his cousins that inevitably end in his own
death in battle; and his ecstasy over the riotous drunks at the summer festival—these spots of time are arrested in cold clear pictures. And there is little intervention by the narrator as he records
these scenes from his childhood, or what he calls his "preamble to
[his] life" (p. 20).

In chapter 2 the "I" is already an adolescent, but still unbur-
dened by the full knowledge of sexuality. Thus, in the scene of
his first masturbation in front of the Saint Sebastian picture, the
"I" is essentially innocent of the meaning of his act. Rather, it is
an immediate experience of sexuality that allows him the pleasure
without the knowledge of "perversity." Such pleasure, an experience of beauty really and one still unpolluted by knowledge and
guilt, is granted him only a little longer. His erotic vision of the
ocean as he dreams of Ōmi (pp. 86–87) is one of the few really
beautiful passages in the book, because his observation, clear of
worrisome self-consciousness, allows him to respond sensuously
and immediately with a remarkable freedom from the distortions
of analysis and introspection. The scene ends in masturbation
(this time involving, almost incredibly, his own armpits), yet still
glows with innocence.

By the time Sonoko makes her appearance, however, his time
of grace is over: knowledge and doubt have begun to torment him.
All pleasure, all experience of beauty, must now be dissected in
terms of other relationships. His indifference to women is now
"impotence"; his autoeroticism "inversion"; and his male friendship "perversity." Instead of the pure experience of pleasure and
beauty, a gnawing doubt and anxiety seek to name and evaluate
it, with the inevitable consequence that the edges of experience
itself are dulled and obscured. The "I's" innocence is irrevocably
lost.

It is absurd to see *Confessions of a Mask* as simply a record of
a young homosexual, almost as absurd as calling *Lolita* a memoir
of a child molester. There is a certain aspect of loneliness that only
a sexual pathology can accurately shape. Thus homosexuality and
autoeroticism in Mishima's work are not allowed to be the end-

meaning of the story, but are made to serve as metaphors. What is more, the worry over one's perversion can serve as a fit metaphor for a knowledge, only gradually and painfully attained, of the transience of childhood and the passage of time. There is an intense sadness to this loss reverberating far beneath and beyond the author's personal life.

There are two further aspects of the *Confessions* that need at least brief discussion: first, its aristocratic setting, and second, the background of the War.

Upper-class experience is no doubt a fact of Mishima's personal life. But in this work, the life style of privileged families—with their numerous servants and regular summer vacations—is not so obtrusively center stage as it often is in later works. To be sure, the connections and friendships developed at the "I's" school— Gakushūin, obviously, though not identified as such—are an integral part of the work, just as they were very important to Mishima personally in his youth. And yet even in this novel, there is already at work an extraordinary sensibility regarding class distinctions. The boy's sexual response to the nightsoil man, for instance, is not just one example of a rich kid's romantic sympathy for the poor and underprivileged; there is something more psychological here, resembling a masochistic identification. One may note, in this connection, that the youngster's friendships are exclusively with other students of the same school, and yet the narrator is completely silent about the relatively inferior position he must have held within the group itself, a clique known for its morbidly acute sense of social hierarchy and characterized as such in the book itself. More important, the narrator chooses to talk of things and experiences belonging exclusively to this class. The reference inventory of *Confessions of a Mask* gives its territory an aura as artificial and romantic as that of any Camelot. With Mishima—even more so than with Dazai—devotion to the aristocratic life style is pure pastoral wish-fulfillment, but it is also a defensive tactic which would manipulate the unwary into suspending some important critical responses. If it works here, it is because the young hero's behavior is not so different from that of an ordinary middle-class youth. At times, especially in those novels serialized in the women's magazines, Mishima is downright vulgar in

the way he hands over the sagas of aristocrats—almost like fan
magazine exposés of the semi-scandalous lives of movie stars of
whom the reader is assumed to have no intimate knowledge at all.
And while we understand that the "aristocratic" setting is in some
sense Mishima's way of presenting more and greater possibilties
for life than those allowed by middle-class experience—his equivalent of Ōgai's "imported life"—we also get the feeling he may be
playing with fire.

Indeed, this snobbishness was more damaging to Mishima's
work than he realized. Take the scene in which the narrator has
just returned from a visit to Sonoko's brother. He arrived back in
Tokyo on March 10, 1945, the morning after the great air raid
that destroyed overnight the larger part of downtown Tokyo, a
district mainly populated by working-class families. Here is the
narrator's observation:

> I was emboldened and strengthened by the parade of mis-
> ery passing before my eyes. I was experiencing the same
> excitement that a revolution causes. In the fire these mis-
> erable ones had witnessed the total destruction of every
> evidence that they existed as human beings. Before their
> eyes they had seen human relationships, loves and hatreds,
> reason, property, all go up in flame. And at the time it had
> not been the flames against which they fought, but against
> human relationships, against loves and hatreds, against
> reason, against property. At the time, like the crew of a
> wrecked ship, they had found themselves in a situation
> where it was permissible to kill one person in order that
> another might live. A man who died trying to rescue his
> sweetheart was killed, not by the flames, but by his sweet-
> heart; and it was none other than the child who murdered
> its own mother when she was trying to save it. The condi-
> tion they had faced and fought against there—that of a
> life for a life—had probably been the most universal and
> elemental that mankind ever encounters. (Pp. 160–61)

The sophistry of the passage is quite poisonous. By this view, the
suffering survivors are in fact victors in a war, a war for survival
of one against another, the disaster having brought out these

"universal and elemental" conditions of man's existence. Is man then more truly himself when warring with his fellow man? The perversity of such a view, presented here almost as an epiphany, is achieved only by practicing a determined aloofness from others. And that distance, we must remember, is the design-specified foreground of Mishima's literary architecture, which is to add one structure after another in the next twenty years.*

The war affects the work in several ways. For one, the relationship of the "I" and Sonoko would not have developed at all had the hero not felt his impending death. Death, after all, condenses more of the future into the present moment. But more important, his feeling for the parts of the past now irrevocably lost is also tied to his sense of imminent death. Sudden violent death is beautiful, too, because it is unknown, but also because it cuts people down while they are still full of possibility. Death can rescue one from ugly decline, and preserve one forever in the garden of innocence.

The narrator escaped his own dying at this point, but not the threat and charm of death. The war ought to have killed him and saved him from his future: such regret is inextricably there in the book's mourning over the passage of time and beauty. Likewise Mishima Yukio who survived the war seems to have lived through the postwar years in mourning for the death denied him. This heightened sense of death only possible during war never leaves Mishima's mind. Viewed this way, his suicide is a revenge on the war that did not provide him his end at that youthful time.

During the seven years between *Confessions of a Mask* and *The Temple of the Golden Pavilion* (1956), Mishima wrote several plays, short stories, essays, and as many as eleven novels. Of the three published in 1950, *Thirst for Love* (*Ai no Kawaki*; translated into English in 1969) is the best, although the Mauriac-like obsession with passion and death is peculiarly qualified by its homosexual sensibility. Several people have commented on the similiarity of the heroine's sexual feeling toward her servant-lover

---

* In the aforementioned interview with Akiyama Shun in January, 1968, for instance, he refers to the same air raid experience and asserts that his literature began to develop out of the feeling of gladness that while others had been killed, he had survived (p. 89).

and the "I's" relationship to men in *Confessions of a Mask*. *The Blue Period* (*Ao no Jidai*), based on an actual event, is in many ways a forerunner of *The Temple of the Golden Pavilion*. Into the persona of a brilliant undergraduate briefly successful as a usurer, Mishima projects his quasi-Nietzschean world-system, thus experimenting with a kind of philosophical novel.

Forbidden Colors (*Kinjiki* and *Higyō*) was published in two parts in 1951 and 1952–53 (translated into English in 1968). Continuing the homosexual preoccupation of the *Confessions*, this novel is one of the gaudiest and emptiest Mishima ever wrote. The relationship between the handsome young man and his aging mentor is straight out of *Dorian Gray* but lacks Wilde's charm and world-weariness. The old man's use of his protégé to retaliate against the women in his past is embarrassingly sentimental. In the second part, one detects Mishima's recent reading of Thomas Mann, especially *Death in Venice,* and throughout there appear passages reading like a Takarazuka libretto simulating Tokyo high society.

Mishima knew its failure,[6] and his next work, *The Sound of Waves* (*Shiosai,* 1954), shows his effort to purge his writing of this artificiality. A deliberately simple love story set in a fishing village, it is in a way his challenge to Kawabata's "The Izu Dancer." In his next book, *The Sunken Waterfall* (*Shizumeru Taki,* 1955), Mishima returns to his more sophisticated interests: a brilliant, rich, and handsome civil engineer, tired of easy women, runs into a genuinely frigid one—to his delight and refreshment. He falls in love, and the woman, too, begins to thaw. But to keep his ecstasy at a fine pitch, he goes away for a six-month winter stay at a remote dam site. Despite their serious attachment to each other, the war of nerves goes on until she is unable to contain herself and leaves her husband for him. But her surrender revolts him and this time he freezes. Just as her husband arrives to take her home, she drowns herself. The place where she dies, the waterfall of the title, is itself submerged as the dam is completed and a deep reservoir is formed. Mishima's plots do not outline well as a rule, and this story is perhaps less absurd in its fullness than the digest might suggest. Yet the thinness of characterization in this work, too, mars its apparent intention to present a type of new hero for the technological age.

The Temple of the Golden Pavilion (*Kinkakuji*) was serialized at the rate of a chapter a month from January to October of 1956. The story was based on an act of arson committed by a mad Zen acolyte in the summer of 1950, but it is important not to make too much of that fact. Mishima borrowed only the barest report of the event, which he then used as a scaffolding for his own characterization and notions of motivation. Much more than *The Blue Period*—or even *After the Banquet* and *Silk and Insight* of later years—*The Temple of the Golden Pavilion* unfolds Mishima's unique vision of the world which has almost nothing to do with the facts of the actual event which instigated it.

The Golden Temple—to shorten the title—is, again, in the first person. Whereas *Confessions of a Mask* somehow maintains the form of a "confession," the narrator confiding his inner events as if in a diary, *The Golden Temple* is a much more indefinite soliloquy. Here the arsonist Mizoguchi is presumably telling his story after having committed the crime. But nothing is said about his present whereabouts (is he in prison?), his listener's identity, or about the circumstances giving rise to his soliloquy. (Compare Nabokov's careful, if tongue-in-cheek, setting of the narrative situation in *Lolita*.) Is his narrative meant to be a written document? If so, who is his intended reader? In one passage, for instance, Mizoguchi directly addresses this reader/listener, asking him to remember the way he (Mizoguchi) felt at his father's funeral.[7] But even here his idea of this audience is quite unclear. Who is it? Such vagueness in Mishima's central conception of the narrative situation says a good deal about the work.

The story is told from the viewpoint of the man who has already burned down the Golden Temple. But is his voice (as he relates scenes from his boyhood, for instance) sufficiently modulated by the later experience? Does the work take account of the temporal distance between the earlier boyhood experience, the narrator's pivotal act of destruction, and the present act of narration itself? What was said as regards the *Confessions* must be repeated here, and even more emphatically: this work, too, evades consequentiality by the most subtle means. What happened earlier is connected with what comes later only thematically, not novelistically—that is, not historically, psychologically, or causally.

For evidence of this, it is notable that the narrator's sophisticated aesthetics has no endorsement in his experience. Nothing thus far in his background would have been likely to develop such a high degree of articulation on the meaning of beauty. (I am not insisting that Mizoguchi's aesthetics is "incredible," given his origins and education, but am arguing that *The Golden Temple* simply disregards the job of making it appear probable or even feasible in the light of his background.) The limits of his knowledge and consciousness are quite arbitrarily drawn according to the situation at hand. On the occasion of his picnic with Kashiwagi and the girls, for instance, the narrator refers to a *noh* play, and there is nothing in the book to support his familiarity with this esoteric art. A more serious matter, the narrator's sanity is temporarily in doubt at one point, the purpose of this ambiguity being far from clear. As he goes to the brothel (in chap. 9), he fantasizes that Uiko, long dead, is "still alive" (p. 222). Is Mizoguchi really under the illusion of her being alive? Or is he merely *imagining?* The narrator's comments are of little help: "While Uiko was still alive, I had felt that she was able to go freely in and out of a double world of this kind. . . . Perhaps for Uiko death had been merely a temporary incident" (p. 225). One recalls no indication whatever of such thoughts about the girl earlier. Are we to understand then that Mizoguchi is too far gone into his schizophrenic withdrawal to keep clear about things like who is alive and who is dead? Doesn't his insanity—be it the case—change the book's reading of the hero as a philosopher of beauty with brilliant insights, though admittedly nihilistic and perverse? Either way, Mizoguchi as a full novelistic character is at best dubious.

It is tempting to generalize here and talk about Mishima's overall failure in characterization. There is no question that he created very few memorable characters. Perhaps he is "too much himself" to feel with other people, to become them, as a character-novelist might do. But to point out what a writer cannot do very well is only a very small part of criticism. He is what he is because of other things which he does uniquely and other writers may not do nearly as well or at all. We must look elsewhere than in characterization for Mishima's accomplishment.

It is surprising that there is hardly any good full treatment of this book, which has attracted so much attention in its English translation. The author of the Introduction to Ivan Morris's translation, for instance, seems to take it as a dramatic novel whose hero is afflicted with a "sick mind" (p. x). Although she reverses this somewhat in saying the work is "free of judgment" (p. xi), she views *The Golden Temple* by and large as a "Dostoevskian" look into a psychopath's act of destruction. Of course this is patently absurd, and, probably sensing the shortcomings of such remarks, she escapes into an all too easy refuge: "[It] could only have been written by a Japanese" (p. xviii). The impenetrable East! Nakamura Mitsuo, in a review published in 1956, is shrewd enough to detect the "ghost of the I-novel tradition" in this work by a self-proclaimed opponent of that tradition. Calling the arsonist's action inevitable only "logically" or "ideologically," he finds the "I" of the novel quite devoid of "internal development," not a young man alive but "the author's idea of youth." Similarly, the critic argues, in omitting all mention of the simple moral question involved in the destruction of the temple, Mishima wipes off all the shabbiness and absurdity from his acolyte and turns an outrageous criminal act into a young aristocrat's intellectual prank.[8]

Another point of view helpful for understanding the book appears in an interview with Mishima in January 1957 conducted by Kobayashi Hideo, known as the dean of Japanese literary criticism. Here Kobayashi suggests that *The Golden Temple* is no novel. Comparing it with *Crime and Punishment*, he observes that Dostoevsky need not be concerned with Raskolnikov's motives, while Mishima must be—since *The Golden Temple* deals with the young man's whole development up to the crime itself— and yet fails to. He goes on to say that, with the book offering no real interpersonal relationship, no real relationship between the hero and society, the hero remains trapped throughout within his own subjective view of his motivation, and that such a book, having no "character," is more a lyrical poem than a novel. Obviously cornered, Mishima switches the topic here, and the two men go on to talk about Dostoevsky, Mozart, talent and genius, and such things for a while. Then, as the conversation drifts back to *The Golden Temple*, Mishima blurts out, as he rarely did in innumerable talks and interviews since, what he sees as the book's intention:

MISHIMA: I wrote about a man, the symbol of the artist, pursued by the idée fixe of beauty. Some critic has told me that it is an artist novel—with not an artist but a priest as its hero, and that that's what makes it unusual and interesting. My intention was something like that.

KOBAYASHI: But I still don't consider it a novel.

MISHIMA: No, no. I understand.[9]

For a true reading of *The Golden Temple*, one must resist the impulse to see it dramatically. Mizoguchi's tale is not a dramatic monologue; nor is it a clinical self-observation of a schizophrenic. But his view of beauty, which recurs in one form or another in all Mishima's works up to the very last, may safely be taken for Mishima's.

The narrator's relationship with the Temple of the Golden Pavilion begins as he builds its image in his mind, solely on the basis of his father's comments. The temple so imagined is as real and complete as is his whole inner world, in which he is shut off from the outside by his stuttering. Between his consciousness and the world in which he lives, there ought to be a bridge of language, but there is not.

When a stutterer is struggling desperately to utter his first sound, he is like a little bird that is trying to extricate itself from thick lime. When finally he manages to free himself, it is too late. To be sure, there are times when the reality of the outer world seems to have been waiting for me, folding its arms as it were, while I was struggling to free myself. But the reality that is waiting

for me is not a fresh reality. When finally I reach the outer world after all my efforts, all that I find is a reality that has instantly changed color and gone out of focus— a reality that has lost the freshness that I had considered fitting for myself, and that gives off a half-putrid odor. (Pp. 5–6)

He is congealed inside himself, and his "solitude grow[s] more and more obese, just like a pig" (p. 9). The "pig" is the temple of his imagination—his curse—and at the same time his existence itself.

His love for Uiko proves but another failed bridge, doomed from the beginning. For as he seemingly runs toward her, he has "made a desperate dash only inside the interior of himself" (p. 11).[10] The girl sees him only as a stutterer who is continually about to speak without being able to. And so completely frozen is he in his speechless internality that he is unable to do anything else either—a failure he will atone for by a destruction which is at least in part an assertion of his relationship to the outside world. If Mizoguchi fails her here, however, so does Uiko fail someone else. Her lover is a deserter whom she betrays to the military police. Mizoguchi feels that by this betrayal she now belongs to him, for they are both outsiders now. But the possibility of such an alliance is illusory. In the violent succeeding scene, the lover, being gunned down by his pursuers, shoots Uiko and kills himself. Mizoguchi remains alone after all, condemned by his stammer to his Temple of the Golden Pavilion.

Yet he is not certain even about the temple now. If the temple is beautiful there in Kyoto, far away, that means it can exist without him and his own existence is "a thing estranged from beauty" (p. 21). How does the temple out there relate to him? When his father takes him to Kyoto to see it, he is rather disappointed: it is "merely a small, dark, old three-storied building" (pp. 24–25). Thus it is not until he returns home in the provinces that the temple comes back to "exist more deeply and more solidly within [him]" (p. 29) than ever before. As of this point, the temple stands, it would seem, only in his inner world.

All of this happens in chapter 1. As in the *Confessions*, Mishima

provides most of the major themes and motifs of the work at the very beginning, although he is unwilling to weave them into any discernible pattern at this point. The connections become more evident to the reader—as they do to the narrator himself—as events unfold later on.

Mizoguchi's move to the temple as an acolyte is not in itself the occasion for a closer tie. It is the threat of the American bombs and the possible consequent destruction of the Golden Temple that accomplishes this. Whereas *Confessions of a Mask* mourned over the passage of time that erodes the experience of beauty, here it is the anticipation of the soon-to-come destruction that intensifies it. "[In] this last summer, in these last summer holidays, on the very last day of them" (p. 44), the "real temple" has now "become no less beautiful than that of [his] mental image" (p. 45). What the stutterer cannot resolve by himself is resolved for him, momentarily, by the all-annihilating war. At this moment, his inner temple and the actual temple remarkably correspond.

It is also under the threat of war that Mizoguchi meets Tsurukawa, who ignores his stammering and becomes his only good friend. The two witness the scene of a soldier taking leave of the woman he loves in a tea ceremony. The sense of imminent death makes their parting seem intensely sexual to the watchers: before their eyes, the woman takes out her breast and expresses her milk into her lover's tea. For Mishima, it seems, the erotic is only possible in the shadow of coming death.

But when the war ends with no damage to either the temple or Mizoguchi, the relationship between the two must again change. For one thing, the building's expression of eternity is now majestically restored.

> Never had the temple displayed so hard a beauty—a beauty that transcended my own image, yes, that transcended the entire world of reality, a beauty that bore no relation to any form of evanescence! Never before had its beauty shone like this, rejecting every sort of meaning. (P. 63)

The actual Golden Temple expands and fills not only its space

but beyond with the substance of all time, the past, present, and future, while it crowds Mizoguchi's inner Golden Temple, his whole congealed inner being, to absolute zero. The country's defeat meant for the "I" nothing more than this personal experience of defeat: peace—death momentarily suspended—severs him from beauty completely.

Mizoguchi's strategy for rebuilding his inner world seems to lie in his acceptance of evil. From the hilltop behind the temple, he views the sea of lights now liberated from the wartime blackout:

> At the thought that these countless lights are all [wicked]
> lights, my heart is comforted. Please let the evil that is
> in my heart increase and multiply indefinitely, so that it
> may correspond in every particular with that vast light
> before my eyes! Let the darkness of my heart, in which
> that evil is enclosed, equal the darkness of the night,
> which encloses those countless lights! (P. 71)

He does not analyze the relationship now in effect between the changed meaning for him of the Golden Temple and his new determination to be wicked. The connection must reveal itself as time—and the story—progresses. His first evil act—helping an Occupation soldier stomp on a prostitute to induce abortion and then concealing the deed from his Superior at the temple—begins to glitter in his memory, as if evil were to take the place there of the shining structure. Also about this time, Kashiwagi, the clubfooted evangelist of evil, is introduced, and the stammerer and the cripple become fast friends in their dark knowledge. What clubfootedness is to Kashiwagi, stammering is to Mizoguchi: both are hemmed in from the outside world by their infirmities. (Kashiwagi's twisted metaphysics of love and lust, reality and appearance, is hard to follow, but then it is not really central to the narrator's development, or the novel's. The one is the other's tutor, yet the two are not really very much alike. Kashiwagi's sadism is not Mizoguchi's; nor is his typical accommodation to life similar in any important respect.)

Twice through Kashiwagi's encouragement the narrator comes close to relating to women: once with a girl Kashiwagi has introduced; another time, with a teacher of flower arrangement, the woman whose goodbye to her lover Mizoguchi had witnessed. On both occasions, however, the temple looms up, rousing itself from its indifferent and incomparable eternity to reduce all his efforts, essentially to nullify life. In such moments, it embraces him as though no gulf at all existed between his restricted inner world and beauty's boundlessness. But its embrace is brief. As he awakens from transport, he knows how he is being separated from life by the capricious Golden Temple. The two are incompatible; in fact they are adversaries. As long as the Golden Temple exists, he is essentially incapacitated for existence. In order to live, he must bring it under his sway and even destroy it.

In the meantime, his life at the temple deteriorates. He neglects his schoolwork. His friend Tsurukawa dies, leaving him all alone except for the black patronage of the crippled philosopher. And the Superior, that enigmatic spiritual guide, becomes totally uncommunicative. In his attempt to "find him out," Mizoguchi repeatedly provokes the older priest, but with little effect. His attempt to penetrate the Superior's "hypocrisy" is wholly frustrated. The contest between the "I's" power of evil and whatever evil may lie in the Superior is one-sided from the beginning. His spiritual father is utterly secure in his corruption, against which Mizoguchi's evil, his substitute Golden Temple, seems to amount to little more than a schoolboy's petulant defiance.

At this point, his trip home becomes a pilgrimage to confirm his existence. In the bleak country of western Japan, which for him is the "source of all [his] unhappiness, of all [his] gloomy thoughts, the origin of all [his] ugliness and all [his] strength" (p. 190), he rediscovers a life without a trace of beauty. It is as if he were baptized anew by the desolation of this, his birthplace, and he knows he must dissolve all beauty into this shapeless ugliness, into the elements of the earth. "I must set fire to the Golden Temple" (p. 191).

The succeeding events only further confirm Mizoguchi's belief in death and destruction. First, Kashiwagi tells him the circumstances of Tsurukawa's death (despite his serene appearance, Tsurukawa, too, was afflicted by misfortune; his death was a suicide). Second, when Mizoguchi visits a brothel, he finds that the memory of Uiko no longer interferes, she is "out" (p. 224); nor does the Golden Temple obtrude any more. He does not even stutter as he talks to the whore. And in that unobstructed relationship with the outside, the "I" has sex with her in a completely routine way. There is only one more task still to be done: he must overcome all doubt about the action. "Having so completely dreamed the deed, having so completely lived that dream, is there any need to act it out physically? Wouldn't such action be quite useless at this stage?" (p. 256). What is the reality finally? Knowledge or action? Does doing add anything to what is known? Will the outside confirm the inside? A little over a dozen years later, Mishima must have asked himself the same question, and answered yes. And his Mizoguchi in *The Temple of the Golden Pavilion* said yes, "precisely because it [is] so futile" (p. 258). The Golden Temple burns to ashes in a few moments.

Any synopsis of *The Golden Temple* will necessarily ignore the apparent irrelevancies that deepen and enrich it, and will, unfortunately, impose logic on a work which in many respects resists logic. Clearly, nothing substitutes for reading the novel itself and experiencing its whole texture. Although threading the various strands into a pattern is often a helpful exercise, such a reading still will not yield a clear outline. Several nagging questions need to be heard. What happens to beauty by the burning of the Golden Temple? And how does it affect the future of the "I's" relationship with the outside world? Also important, in what way does the arsonist "symbolize the artist"?

That no beauty exists without constant threat of perishing is a given of this book. As long as the bombing continues, the "I" is at ease with the Golden Temple—in love with it, really—feeling no gap between the mind's image and the actual structure. The moment the danger disappears, beauty loses its evanescence, and it now belongs to a different order. The "I" must restore the danger so that equilibrium can be restored between external beauty and his inner world in all its vulnerability.

There is also the problem of beauty's destructive force over life. Because the Golden Temple is ordered into an exquisite form, it rejects the chaos that life is. And the perceiver, if unable at the same time to bear with the disorder and shapelessness of life, must either reject experience totally or shut his eyes to the form that exists only in lifeless art. To escape the paradox, the "I" finds another way: he will destroy the form in order to be released from its spell; in this way he feels he can at least live, even if his life is consequently disordered and unbeautiful. Action, whatever its particular nature, at least has this faculty of reclaiming life over sterile order.

Let us now look at Mizoguchi as an artist. Pursued by his vision of beauty, the stutterer repeatedly tries to confirm it in the world out there and repeatedly fails. Is his beauty the same as the world's beauty then? The gnawing feeling never leaves him that the two have at least a very tenuous connection. His beauty is, after all, his alone. But even when it adequately sustains his inner world—at the expense of his participation in life—it always fails him crucially in the face of the insistent actual. Unable to taste the ordinary pleasures of life and also frustrated in sustaining a continuous ecstatic relationship with beauty, the "I" is utterly alone in his desolation. Neither the resonant silence of the Golden Temple nor the ordinary stir of human life can be heard in this no man's land where his stammer alone interminably hisses and gasps its non-meaning on the dead air. What's worse, this stammer—the artist's very means of art—is a curse that will never be lifted from him. He stands eternally condemned by his own art.

Burning the Golden Temple may be a mad act even for an artist, since obliteration of the temple does nothing to guarantee the authenticity of his inner vision. But still, coexistence is impossible, and as his logic goes, he imagines his act of destruction may do something to change other people's awareness of beauty. Since the order that makes beauty possible consists in the end of disordered matter, the reduction of the form to its chaotic components ought to make people realize beauty's ultimate nothingness. Indeed, it should make the artist himself realize that his efforts to prove that his vision is more than nothing are also futile. Meanwhile, the Golden Temple is something: an obese pig that grows and grows inside him, feeding on what remains of his isolated self.

Finally, the portrait of the artist emerging from *The Temple of the Golden Pavilion* is almost totally negative, with little in it to justify either the artist's craft or his vision. Only the near-mad act of total devastation generates any meaning for the artist. But then, Mishima's art is seldom a cheerful one. He raises questions, disturbing, destructive ones, for which he is uninterested in finding answers. *The Temple of the Golden Pavilion* is a dangerous, disturbing, and beautiful book mostly because beauty really is dangerous, existing only where life itself is threatened with annihilation.

Mishima was thirty-one when he wrote *The Temple of the Golden Pavilion*. Within three years he had built a new home, a hodgepodge "Victorian Rococo," and married. His home life was highly regulated: he woke up at noon, spent the afternoon working out physically, entertained his friends in the evening, and wrote from midnight to dawn. Undoubtedly such a strict routine contributed to his enormous output of plays, essays, pamphlets, and novels.

Many if not most of the fifteen novels written between *The Temple of the Golden Pavilion* and the tetralogy are remarkably trivial. Some could be soap opera scripts. *Too Long a Spring* (*Nagasugita Haru*, 1956) recounts a young couple's ups and downs during their year-long engagement. In *The Tottering Virtue* (*Bitoku no Yoromeki*, 1957) a bored upper-class housewife has an affair. *The Young Lady* (*Ojōsan*, 1960) is the nondescript tale of a corporation executive's daughter getting married, becoming jealous, and then happily pregnant. *The Scamper of Love* (*Ai no Shissō*, 1962), a feeble experiment in double narrative, tells of a provincial author who writes of the love of a young working-class couple. *The School of Flesh* (*Nikutai no Gakkō*, 1963), a popularized version of *Forbidden Colors*, has a rich divorcée befriending a cool bisexual. *Music* (*Ongaku*, 1964) is a quasi-Freudian account of a frigid girl unable to "hear music." *A Complicated Man* (*Fukuzatsuna Kare*, 1966) tells of an uncomplicated airline steward's love for a rich girl and his sudden change of heart at the end. In *The Evening Dress* (*Yakaifuku*, 1966–67) former aristocrats and royalty brighten up the story of a rich young couple's marriage. Finally, *A Life for Sale* (*Inochi*

Urimasu), published as late as 1968, is the story of a quasi-Mafia organization, complete with a female vampire. They are, every one of them, practically worthless, but probably the worst thing about them is that Mishima seems utterly contemptuous in them of his readers, tossing out what he told himself they wanted. I do not know what commercial success these publications brought him, but critically, at any rate, the less said the better.

Of several more interesting works, *Kyōko's Home* (*Kyōko no Ie*, 1958–59) deserves mention. Kyōko, a rich divorcée, is friends with four different men, who represent four aspects of Mishima's self-image: a businessman who is also an eschatologist, an artist, an actor, and a boxer. "Kyōko" means "mirror girl," and the novel is intended to be a reflection of postwar Japan. Here Mishima is trying for once to look panoramically at the whole society. The book, overly discursive and lacking in full characterization, fails as a novel, but it does show the author's serious intention to confront broad social problems.[11] As he confessed to Ōshima Nagisa, the film director, nearly ten years later, he was shocked by the lack of response to this work. "I am a bit embarrassed to say this, but I wanted the book to be understood by everyone. I was going to throw my baby into the river, as it were. I was waiting for someone to stop me. But no one came. In despair, I threw it. That was the end. Of me. It's all finished. I am not yet arrested. So I'm doing all sorts of things now to get caught. The coldness of the literary world, then! . . . I must have gone mad ever since."[12] It is interesting that Mishima's overtly subversive "politics" dates from the time of *Kyōko's Home*.

After the Banquet (*Utage no Ato*, 1960), translated into English in 1963, is based on an actual Tokyo mayoralty campaign and is one of the most unified of his works. It is also unique in presenting fully drawn characters. The heroine's tenacious optimism and will to live are rare qualities in Mishima's usually bored and frigid population. *The Play of Beasts* (*Kemono no Tawamure*, 1961) and *Beautiful Stars* (*Utsukushii Hoshi*, 1962) are both moderately experimental works: the former, for dealing with complex ideas of death, crime, and love in a compact setting;

the latter, for its use of the conventions of science fiction. *Beautiful Stars* is also especially interesting as an eschatological reading of the fate of the earth.

The Towing in the Afternoon (*Gogo no Eikō*, 1963), translated into English as *The Sailor Who Fell from Grace with the Sea* in 1965, is in my view the best of his work after the *Confessions* and *The Golden Temple*. Its teen-age hero, an accomplished voyeur, spies on his mother as she has an affair with a sailor. In the original title, *Gogo no* means "in the afternoon," and *Eikō*, "towing," while its sound suggests "glory." The sailor, for a time the boy's mythical hero, loses this status ("grace with the sea") when he becomes an ordinary landlocked householder. The story relates the boy's revenge on the sailor for destroying the myth, and his attempt to revive it by means of a ritual murder with the help of his gang of brilliant delinquents. Its language is concise, and its imagery—if unremittingly gory in certain passages—is clear and impressive. Even Mishima's frequent plot-flabbiness is nowhere apparent here. It may be a bit too neat and terse, although it is innocent of many of the more usual weaknesses that often mar his novels.

Silk and Insight (*Kinu to Meisatsu*, 1964), another work based on an actual event, describes a textile factory strike. Although one recognizes in the old-fashioned patriarch Mishima's efforts to open a new path in his art, the character is stereotyped and uninteresting. Where *After the Banquet* succeeds in building solid characters, this novel reverts to his usual schematic abstractions.

His tetralogy, *The Sea of Fertility* (*Hōjō no Umi*), was published over five years between September 1965 and January 1971. The work as a whole traces the observations and experiences of Honda Shigekuni, who is an undergraduate in Part One and an old man in Part Four. The first volume, *Spring Snow* (*Haru no Yuki*), translated into English in 1972, concerns itself mainly with the love affair between Honda's friend, Matsugae Kiyoaki, a marquis' son, and Ayakura Satoko, the daughter of an earl. The romance intensifies after the girl becomes affianced to a prince and, in defiance of the Imperial taboo, the young Matsugae insists on continuing to see her. She becomes pregnant and, having sought refuge with the Imperial Abbess, decides to become a nun herself. Failing in his desperate attempts to see her, Matsugae becomes ill and dies. The romance is told in a dazzlingly rich prose carrying a strong nostalgia for the courtly life of the last years of Emperor Meiji's reign.

The second volume, *Runaway Horses* (*Homba*), translated into English in 1973, jumps ahead twenty years to the early 1930s. Honda, now a judge in the Court of Appeals, comes to know the son of a right-wing agitator who was once a houseboy at the Matsugaes'. The young man, a radical patriot like his father, has three moles under the left armpit, just as the young Matsugae did, and Honda becomes convinced that he is the reincarnation of his dead friend. The youth plans a coup d'état with other extreme nationalists. Their conspiracy is uncovered, and he is arrested. Honda, now convinced of the transmigration, resigns his judgeship to defend him, and wins the case. Within a few days of his release, however, the young man assassinates one of the most prominent financial giants of the empire and escapes to commit harakiri alone. Mishima's by now confirmed aesthetic of bloody suicide and belief in the quasi-mystical ways of the samurai are both evident in this work, which he apparently thought of as the "masculine" counterpart to the "feminine" sensibility prevalent in the romance of volume 1.

In the third volume, *The Temple of Dawn* (*Akatsuki no Tera*), Honda is a successful lawyer. In Thailand on a business trip, he is introduced to the young Princess Ying Chan ("Moonlight"), daughter of a Thai prince he once entertained with Matsugae (in vol. 1). The princess, coincidentally a fanatic Japanophile, appears to him as still another resurrection of the friend of his youth. The war breaks out soon after his return to Japan and when it is over, Honda, who has become a millionaire, builds a sumptuous summer home and invites the now grown-up princess to visit him there. Despite many schemes, he fails to win her affection and is reduced to peeking through a secret hole in his study to see her make love to another woman friend of his. That night, a fire breaks out and reduces the villa to ashes. Years later, as an old man he learns that the princess died back home of cobra venom. This is the weakest part of the four volumes. There are several inconsistencies surrounding the Thai princess; the many incidents rushed through at the end—the lesbian affair, the fire, and the princess's death—appear ill-timed and arbitrary; and in its whole conception the Thai episode is not well articulated with the rest. Perhaps in an effort to fuse the work, Mishima devotes a good many pages to lecturing about theories of metempsychosis as if writing for an encyclopedia.

The last volume, *The Decay of the Angel* (*Tennin Gosui*), is the most ingenious. The Matsugae-terrorist-Ying Chan transmigration enters still another phase, when Honda discovers an orphan in a fishing village with the same three moles and adopts him. This boy, a typical Mishima egoist, turns out to be a false incarnation and, soon recognizing his power over his wealthy adoptive father, proceeds to scheme against him. Told the reason for his adoption, the boy tries suicide but falls short and succeeds only in blinding himself. Old Honda is now alone and, feeling the approach of death, visits the Abbess of Gesshū Temple, who was once Ayakura Satoko, the girl Matsugae was in love with. Though now eighty-three, she is still beautiful. But as Honda recalls the days of their youth, she tells him she has never known a Matsugae Kiyoaki. "If Kiyoaki never existed from the beginning," mumbles Honda, "then Isao too didn't exist, nor Ying Chan. Furthermore, possibly even I myself . . ." The Abbess gazes at him intently and says, "That too depends on the way you think." As she shows him the garden of the temple, Honda hears the sound of absolute silence.

> It is a gracious, bright garden with no special artifice. The place is full of the cries of cicadas that sound as though many worshipers were telling their rosaries. There is not a single sound otherwise in the extreme tranquility. There is nothing in the garden. I have come, Honda thought, to a place where there is no memory, nor anything else.
> The garden is quiet in the full summer sun. . . .[13]

The ending thus reverses and obliterates the myth of metempsychosis so elaborately unfolded in these four volumes. But the final passage is meant also to punctuate Mishima's entire career, his entire life. It is not just the matter that the date given for the completion of the tetralogy was chosen as the day of his suicide. But there is the haunting feeling that the last scene of *The Sea of Fertility,* describing a silence that evacuates even memory, seems to be an epitaph Mishima would choose for himself.

The Sea of Fertility is not finally a satisfying novel. Its passion is not the passion of art, but the passion of life. So many impulses tear at the work, the craving for eternal youth—by metempsychosis, if by no other way—and the knowledge of the sure arrival of age, for instance. But even more fundamentally, its clearly Eastern theme and setting, its Meiji aristocracy and exotic Thai temples and palaces, reveal its maker's plans for export. It is his sales pitch to markets abroad, in which he seems interested mainly in redressing the balance of payments on a once imported product, the novel, and exporting this one to the West. What finally brings the four volumes or parts together is the uncontrollable urge in the work to bring them to a close, the eschatological will to death. So exuberant by now in the foreknowledge of death, Mishima refuses to allow any possible vitality or richness that life might yet bring forth. The stillness that dominates the garden at the end of this long novel is, one realizes, the silence of Mare Fecunditatis, the barren sea on the lifeless surface of the moon.

Mishima was an amazingly consistent person, who never forgot his wartime catechism—the myth of Japan as a ritually ordered state, the samurai way of life characterized by manly courage and feminine grace, and the vision of imminent death as the catalyst of life. Fixated as he was on this early training, Mishima never stopped feeling that he was living a leftover life after the war ended. *Confessions of a Mask* and *The Temple of the Golden Pavilion* each in its own way tells of this longing for the end that ought to have overtaken him. And many of the other works seem attempts at brightening the sickened atmosphere that sooner or later was bound to suffocate the earth.

All his life he despised the passivity of intellectualism and the impotence of democracy. Shortly after writing *Kyōko's Home* he developed a program calling for the revival of the warrior's death-threatened way of life in contrast to the all-too-easy life of peace. His grotesque short story "Patriotism" (*Yūkoku,* 1960), minutely describing the suicides of an officer by harakiri and his wife by cutting her throat, preceded by passionate love-making, is one of the earliest works to militarize what would later be a major preoccupation with sado-masochistic death "beautified" by an aesthetic of blood and sexuality. Soon he would begin, too, to be deeply concerned with the "essence" of Japanese culture, and numerous propaganda pieces appeared in rapid succession—a story-essay, "The Voices of the Spirits of the Lost Heroes" (*Eirei no Koe,* 1966), advocating resurrection of the principle of the Divine Emperor, and pamphlets such as *Spiritual Lectures for the Young Samurai* (*Wakaki Samurai no tameni,* 1968–69), *An Introduction to Action Philosophy* (*Kōdōgaku Nyūmon,* 1969), and *The Theory of Patriotism* (*Yūkoku no Genri,* 1970). It should be remembered that these were years when Japan was shaken by a great number of social and political crises signaled by a nearly endless series of demonstrations and protests. Compared with those in the United States in the sixties, the Japanese demonstrations were many times larger in force and scale. They were more massively organized and far more efficiently disciplined, and their cry of outrage—against, say, the Japan–United States Mutual Security Pact—was focused and demonstrably effective. Mishima was a frequent participant in university debates and teach-ins, always leaping into the turbulence from the side of the extreme right-wing.* In all his battles, he seems to have been convinced that a revolution was imminent —probably in 1970—and he himself was ready to fight—with,

---

* His single-handed debate with the assembled students of the University of Tokyo is published in *Mishima Yukio versus the Strike Coalition Committee of the University of Tokyo* (*Mishima Yukio–Tōdai Zenkyōtō*) (Tokyo: Shinchōsha, 1969). Some of his views are similar to those expressed by hostile critics of university affairs during the 1960s in the United States. The tone is suggested by the title of one essay, "Turn the University of Tokyo into a Zoo" (*Tōdai o Dōbutsuen ni Shiro*), collected in *Spiritual Lectures for the Young Samurai* (Tokyo: Nippon Kyōbunsha, 1969). Yet Mishima and the striking radical students seem to have found common ground in their rejection of the "hypocritical," "liberal" administrations of the universities and the nation. He reportedly said at the time that he felt warm toward the students and would join them if only they would accept the principle of the divine Imperial order.

characteristically, his own ancient sword in his hand and his hand-groomed corps of handsome young swordsmen at his side. He dreamed of revolution, because it would have served him in a way as a second chance. And as 1970 passed into its second half without any sign of general insurrection, he had to plan and stage one of his own.

Read as political statements, the books leading up to his last act are fantasies. Over and over again Mishima advocates the way of the samurai, and pleads for a revival of the kamikaze spirit as if the pilots were martyrs for beauty and sanctity. Though full of the images of *Blut und Boden,* the books fail to set out a coherent politics. In fact he carefully avoids identification with any recent fascism. His play *My Friend Hitler (Waga Tomo Hitler,* 1968), for example, is not quite the fanatic endorsement suggested by the title and appearance of the book (the wrapper with Hitler's portrait, and the black binding complete with swastika). The *Führer* of the play is an aesthete trying to survive the game of black politics and still needing lessons from the foxier Herr Gustav Krupp. If this does not exactly mitigate what amounts to a vulgar diabolism on the part of Mishima, the play is at the same time certainly no apology for the demented Nazi. Also, in his supposedly political manifestoes, his thoughts continually dwell on the idea of death. (*The Introduction to Action Philosophy,* for example, devotes more than half its length to a series of brief eschatological essays on the "end" of things, like "The End of the Hero," or "The End of the World.") And even in his proposals for the reconstitution of Japan, he is totally indifferent to the economics either of wealth or of power. Thus, having nothing to offer as a political program except the revival of a defunct Imperial order, his criticism both of capitalism and communism is historically a piece of nonsense.

Mishima was of course the embodiment of the unpolitical. Unless one takes "being unpolitical" as itself a political position (as it is in most contexts where politics is broadly construed), his program was organized by the kind of sensibility that is indifferent if not thoroughly antagonistic to the drives and aspirations of actual politics. His lack of interest in planning for the follow-up stages of his own program testifies to its essentially visionary quality. The "coup d'état" he had so carefully planned—presumably to catalyze certain counterrevolutionary elements in Japan's National Self-Defence Force—amounted politically to no more than a ceremonial dance performed in honor of something quite unrelated to politics. In all Japanese history, in fact, there has been no attempted coup that was more scrupulously staged to produce a null effect. It was as if he had done his best to ensure that this time he would be able to finish what the war disastrously failed to finish for him. Although he no doubt saw through the illusions of those who see modern Japanese culture as essentially "Western," and although he probably intended to present a serious alternative, what he came up with is no less a fantasy than what he would replace. For what he called the "culture, history, and tradition" of Japan became in the end little more than his own personal mythology, and his last "political" act merely demonstrated the essential tautology of his life: what he had always demanded of life was something so valuable one can only pay for it with one's life.

Mishima may have considered suicide quite often since adolescence, but he became really serious about it during his last few years. There were hints of this in a number of interviews he had with other writers, but no one at that time took them for what they were. In one such talk, recorded only a week before he died, he is unusually serene and lucid as he recalls and analyzes his long writing career and explains his present politics. Referring very generally to the action he knows he is about to take in a few days, he remarks how exhausted he is and jokes about how he may be "finished" as a writer, having said all he can think of saying and being unable to make any plans for the future.[14] Then, in a more subdued mood, he recalls how his "self-formation" was completed by the time he was "fifteen or sixteen, at the latest nineteen," and in a moment of rare self-revelation, he calls his recent "Romanticism" a *"Heimkehr* [his word, home-coming] to his teen-age" (p. 167). It is clear he is aware of the circle drawing to a close. He is now where he was once in his youth. He knows too, by this time, that he is in art where he is in life: the two places are identical. And if this means that he—like so many other practitioners of the novel in Japan—could not help confusing life with art, perhaps that problem was of no great concern to him any longer. He was close at last to what he had always wanted. Death was finally something he could pay for with his own life.[15]

Mishima's suicide, like that of Kawabata and Dazai, carries an important social meaning that may help us understand something about the death wish operating throughout modern Japanese literature.*

Earlier, I talked about the poverty of real content in Japanese life, and argued that the novel as a middle-class art form demands more richness and variety in experience than is normally supplied the writer in Japan. I also talked about the underdevelopment of character in Japanese fiction, and how it is rooted in the Japanese hostility toward personality. The Japanese writer must somehow hammer out a personality for himself which he essentially must hide from view since he is not encouraged to express it; and he must fabricate lives in fiction which neither he nor his reader really know at firsthand and which thus lack the authenticity demanded by the novel. Further, as the artist shapes the self and takes it into account, so he must learn ways of ignoring it too at times, if he is to be the kind of artist envisioned by the objectivists. Few are able to. Kawabata managed it by retiring early to the silent margins of life. Mishima craved the absolute, but his own strange god turned out to be the nothingness of death itself.

And there is an even more formidable trial for the Japanese writer, the language itself that discourages formation of tangible individuals and a distinctly personal experience. It does this espe-

---

* Some readers may recall Gore Vidal's article on Mishima and his answer to Ivan Morris's criticism of it (*New York Review of Books,* June 17 and December 16, 1971) in which he poked fun at both Mishima and Professor Morris. Elegantly wrong on several points, Vidal stated, for example, that "Japan's most popular (and deeply admired) writer has been W. Somerset Maugham" (June 17, p. 8), and that Mishima's death was "entirely idiosyncratic, more Western in its romanticism than Japanese" (p. 10). (Did Mr. Vidal, this one time, cruise with the wrong crowd?) Yet I must agree with him that what is finally most fascinating about Mishima is not his work but his life: what he was, what he did, and what he meant in the context of modern Japanese literature.

cially by its tendency to omit the subject, especially the first-person pronominal subject, in its sentences; by its extraordinary development of the honorific system; by its writing medium whose ideograms resist being spoken aloud; and by its loose syntactic form that baffles straightforward statement. Furthermore, as we saw, the language is severely ritualistic and ceremonial, particularly in its dedication to silence. Mishima was one of the best technicians of prose style, and yet his achievements there lay largely in the correctness and orthodoxy of his usage. He never succeeded in matching the language to the strong personal identity he managed to develop. Loose and adaptive as it may appear, Japanese is iron-tight once the speaker violates the rites of community and the sanctity of silence. He must learn to hum along very measuredly as he performs the ceremonial dance, or his speech will become a shriek, or a futile stammer. Kawabata learned this language of silence to perfection—at the expense of his personality; Dazai embarrassed the language with his clowning, until finally it embarrassed him to death; Mishima, who understood the problem better than anyone, had to turn to his body as his "second language." *Sun and Steel* (*Taiyō to Tetsu*, 1968), presents the clearest statement of this option:

> As I pondered the nature of that "I," I was driven to the conclusion that the "I" in question corresponded precisely with the physical space that I occupied. What I was seeking, in short, was a language of the body.[16]

The body can dance, it can kill, and it can die, but it never speaks words. His body disemboweled itself, and through this deed, enacted in his "second language" in homage to his god, he felt he could speak to the people and be heard by them, despite his contempt for them. This, I believe, is what Mishima himself meant when he told Nakamura Mitsuo in 1967 that "suicide activates a writer's entire works." He also remarked later in the same interview, "suicide is art." [17]

Silence powerfully invites the Japanese. But for the writer, accepting the invitation is always fatal. Mishima knew it as soon as he began to write. From *Confessions of a Mask* to *The Sea of*

Fertility, his fiction was a thin mask veiling the ultimate void. His language was only a stammer repeatedly breaking the awesome quiet of that void that persisted as long as he lived.* And, as he knew at the end, his terrible body speech too was finally an utterance in a mute language.

* A. Alvarez discusses a very similar view of suicide which is held by the dadaists. In the chapter "Dada: Suicide as an Art," in *The Savage God: A Study of Suicide* (London: Weidenfeld and Nicolson, 1971), he writes: "When art is against itself, destructive and self-defeating, it follows that suicide is a matter of course" (p. 189). The anti-art context of dadaism is of course totally different from the "anti-art" stance seen in the Japanese novel. But their effects bear striking resemblances and Alvarez's prognosis for Western literature (the "post-Arnold, post-Eliot" writers) is peculiarly applicable to Japanese writers as well: "The existence of the work of art . . . is contingent, provisional; it fixes the energy, appetites, moods and confusions of experience in the most lucid possible terms so as to create a temporary clearing of calm, and then moves on, or back, into autobiography" (pp. 211–12). Certain Japanese writers today, like Abe Kōbō and Ōe Kenzaburō, seem aware of this though in varying degrees.